# Everything TEEN GIRLS Should Know About the BIBLE

Important Stuff That Can Change Your Life

BARBOUR PUBLISHING™

YOU are the reason we do what we do here at Barbour Publishing. We promise that we will always use our God-given talents to produce content with you in mind—and that we will remain biblically faithful, no matter what.

*Thank you for being the heart of our business.*

---



Written and compiled by Tracy M. Sumner

ISBN 979-8-89151-288-7



Cover Design: Greg Jackson, Thinkpen Design

Published by Barbour Publishing, Inc., 1810 Barbour Drive, Uhrichsville, Ohio 44683, www.barbourbooks.com

*Our mission is to inspire the world with the life-changing message of the Bible.*

Printed in the United States of America.

# Contents

**You know that the Bible is important. . .**

**but you also have questions that deserve answers.**

What exactly is the Bible? Where does it come from? How does it apply to my life today? *Everything Teen Girls Should Know About the Bible* is designed to answer those questions and many more. This fascinating book:

- Describes how the Bible came about, by whom, and when
- Lists key characters, terms, and verses to know and memorize
- Provides an overview of scripture's story through a seven-part outline covering Creation to the End Times
- Gives you details about the life and ministry of the Bible's "Main Man," Jesus Christ
- Provides guidance on how to study God's Word through the "inductive method" of observation, interpretation, and application

Through sixty-six separate books, 1,189 chapters, and hundreds of thousands of words, the Bible shares one extraordinary message: God loves you. From the first chapter of Genesis, where God creates human beings, through the last chapter of Revelation, where God welcomes all people to "take the water of life freely," the Bible proves that God is intimately involved in, familiar with, and concerned about the lives of people. His amazing love is shown in the death of His Son, Jesus Christ, on the cross. That sacrifice for sin allows anyone to be right with God through simple faith in Jesus' work. These truths are found in the pages of scripture.

God's Word is the ultimate source of wisdom, and you'll chart the best course for life by knowing it well. Start today with *Everything Teen Girls Should Know About the Bible*!

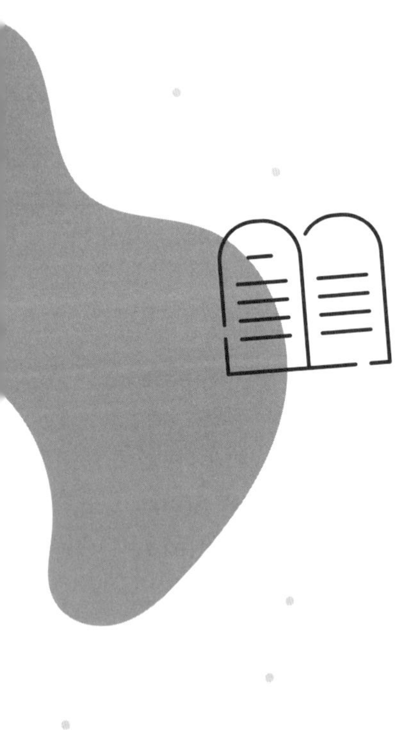

# 1

# Some BIBLE Basics

Here is a great opportunity to learn about the Bible. And not just *facts* about the Bible, though we'll cover plenty of those. In the pages to follow, you'll see what God's Word can do for you, and what it should mean to you.

Let's lay the groundwork by presenting some important basics about the Bible. Want to know more about this incredible gift from God, His written Word? Let's get started!

# Bible Books in Order

The word *Bible* comes from a Latin word meaning "book." Though we often view the Bible as a single book containing the promises, commands, and wisdom of God, it's actually a collection of sixty-six "books," or writings—thirty-nine in the Old Testament and twenty-seven in the New Testament.

Knowing the order of these books as they appear in the Bible is very helpful to your reading and study. So over the next few pages you'll find a list to commit to memory:

## *Old Testament Books*

1. Genesis
2. Exodus
3. Leviticus
4. Numbers
5. Deuteronomy
6. Joshua
7. Judges
8. Ruth
9. 1 Samuel
10. 2 Samuel
11. 1 Kings
12. 2 Kings
13. 1 Chronicles
14. 2 Chronicles
15. Ezra
16. Nehemiah
17. Esther
18. Job
19. Psalms
20. Proverbs
21. Ecclesiastes
22. Song of Solomon
23. Isaiah
24. Jeremiah
25. Lamentations
26. Ezekiel
27. Daniel
28. Hosea
29. Joel
30. Amos
31. Obadiah
32. Jonah
33. Micah
34. Nahum
35. Habakkuk
36. Zephaniah
37. Haggai
38. Zechariah
39. Malachi

# The Bible by the Numbers

- Number of books: 66
- Number of Testaments: 2 (39 books in the Old Testament; 27 in the New)
- Number of writers: around 40
- Number of chapters: 1,189 (929 in the Old Testament; 260 in the New)
- Number of verses: 31,101
- Number of words: around 785,000
- Longest chapter in the Bible: Psalm 119 (176 verses)
- Shortest chapter in the Bible: Psalm 117 (2 verses)

## *New Testament Books*

40. Matthew
41. Mark
42. Luke
43. John
44. Acts
45. Romans
46. 1 Corinthians
47. 2 Corinthians
48. Galatians
49. Ephesians
50. Philippians
51. Colossians
52. 1 Thessalonians
53. 2 Thessalonians
54. 1 Timothy
55. 2 Timothy
56. Titus
57. Philemon
58. Hebrews
59. James
60. 1 Peter
61. 2 Peter
62. 1 John
63. 2 John
64. 3 John
65. Jude
66. Revelation

# Types of Books in the Bible

Interestingly, both the Old and New Testaments contain five different types of writings. Each one serves a specific purpose. The Old Testament includes books of law, history, wisdom and poetry, and prophecy, featuring major and minor prophets (the terms describe the length of their writing, not their relative importance). The New Testament contains the gospels, history of the early church, Paul's epistles, the general epistles, and prophecy. Here is how they break down:

## *Old Testament*

**Law** (5): Genesis, Exodus, Leviticus, Numbers, Deuteronomy

**History** (12): Joshua, Judges, Ruth, 1–2 Samuel, 1–2 Kings, 1–2 Chronicles, Ezra, Nehemiah, Esther

**Wisdom and Poetry** (5): Job, Psalms, Proverbs, Ecclesiastes, Song of Solomon

**Prophecy, Major** (5): Isaiah, Jeremiah, Lamentations, Ezekiel, Daniel

**Prophecy, Minor** (12): Hosea, Joel, Amos, Obadiah, Jonah, Micah, Nahum, Habakkuk, Zephaniah, Haggai, Zechariah, Malachi

### *New Testament*

**Gospels** (4): Matthew, Mark, Luke, John

**History of the Early Church** (1): Acts of the Apostles

**Paul's Epistles** (13): Romans, 1–2 Corinthians, Galatians, Ephesians, Philippians, Colossians, 1–2 Thessalonians, 1–2 Timothy, Titus, Philemon

**General Epistles** (8): Hebrews, James, 1–2 Peter, 1–3 John, Jude

**Prophecy** (1): Revelation

## Summarizing Each Book of the Bible

Bible books, regardless of type, are filled with remarkable promises, challenging commands, and helpful lessons that can help you live out your faith. Here are very brief sketches of what each book is about:

### *Old Testament*

**Genesis**: God creates the world and establishes special nation of people

**Exodus**: God delivers His people, the Israelites, from slavery in Egypt

**Leviticus**: A holy God explains how to worship Him

**Numbers**: Faithless Israelites wander forty years in the wilderness of Sinai

**Deuteronomy:** Moses reminds the Israelites of their history and God's laws

**Joshua**: The Israelites capture and settle the Promised Land of Canaan

**Judges**: Israel goes through cycles of sin, suffering, and delivery through leaders God has chosen

**Ruth**: A loyal daughter-in-law depicts God's faithfulness, love, and care

**1 Samuel**: Israel's twelve tribes unite under a king

**2 Samuel**: David becomes Israel's greatest king, though he has major flaws

**1 Kings**: Israel divides into rival northern and southern kingdoms (Israel and Judah, respectively)

**2 Kings**: Both Jewish nations are destroyed for their disobedience to God

**1 Chronicles**: King David's reign is detailed and analyzed

**2 Chronicles**: The history of Israel—from Solomon, through division, to destruction

**Ezra**: Spiritual renewal begins after the Jews return from exile in Babylon

**Nehemiah**: Returning Jewish exiles rebuild the broken walls of Jerusalem

**Esther**: A beautiful Jewish girl becomes queen of Persia, saving fellow Jews from slaughter

**Job**: God allows human suffering for His own purposes

**Psalms**: The ancient Jewish songbook showcases prayers, praise—and complaints—to God

**Proverbs**: Brief, memorable sayings encourage people to pursue wisdom

**Ecclesiastes**: Apart from God, life is empty and unsatisfying

**Song of Solomon**: Married love is a beautiful thing worth celebrating

**Isaiah**: A coming Messiah will save people from their sins

**Jeremiah**: After years of sinful behavior, Judah will be severely punished

**Lamentations**: A despairing poem about the destruction of Jerusalem

**Ezekiel**: Though Israel is in exile in Babylon, the nation will one day be restored

**Daniel**: Faithful to God in a challenging setting, Daniel is blessed

**Hosea**: A prophet's marriage to an immoral woman reflects God's relationship with wayward Israel

**Joel**: A locust plague pictures God's judgment on His sinful people

**Amos**: Real religion isn't just ritual, but treating people with justice

**Obadiah**: Edom will suffer for participating in Jerusalem's destruction

**Jonah**: A reluctant prophet runs from God and is swallowed by giant fish

**Micah**: Israel and Judah will suffer for their idolatry and injustice

**Nahum**: Powerful, wicked Nineveh will fall before God's judgment

**Habakkuk**: Trust God even when He seems unresponsive or unfair

**Zephaniah**: A coming "day of the Lord" promises heavy judgment

**Haggai**: Jews returning from exile need to rebuild God's temple

**Zechariah**: Jewish exiles should rebuild their temple and anticipate their Messiah

**Malachi**: The Jews have become careless in their attitude toward God

## *New Testament*

**Matthew**: Jesus fulfills the Old Testament prophecies of a coming Messiah

**Mark**: Jesus is God's Son, a suffering servant of all people

**Luke**: Jesus is Savior of all people, whether Jew or Gentile

**John**: Jesus is God Himself, the only Savior of the world

**Acts**: The Holy Spirit's arrival heralds the beginning of the Christian church

**Romans**: Sinners are saved only by faith in Jesus Christ

**1 Corinthians**: An apostle tackles sin problems in the church at Corinth

**2 Corinthians**: Paul defends his ministry to the troubled Corinthian church

**Galatians**: Christians are free from restrictive Jewish laws

**Ephesians**: Christians are all members of Jesus' "body," the church

**Philippians**: "Friendship letter" between the apostle Paul and a beloved church

**Colossians**: Jesus Christ is supreme over everyone and everything

**1 Thessalonians**: Jesus will return to gather His followers to Him

**2 Thessalonians**: Christians should work until Jesus returns

**1 Timothy**: Pastors are taught how to conduct their lives and churches

**2 Timothy**: The apostle Paul's final words to a beloved coworker

**Titus**: Church leaders are instructed on their lives and teaching

**Philemon**: Paul begs for mercy for a runaway slave converted to Christianity

**Hebrews**: Jesus is better than any Old Testament person or sacrifice

**James**: Real Christian faith is shown by one's good works

**1 Peter**: Suffering for the sake of Jesus is noble and good

**2 Peter**: Beware of false teachers within the church

**1 John**: Jesus was real man, just as He is real God

**2 John**: Beware of false teachers who deny Jesus' physical life on earth

**3 John**: Church leaders must be humble, not proud

**Jude**: Beware of heretical teachers and their dangerous doctrines

**Revelation**: God will judge evil and reward His saints

# Important Terms to Remember

When you read and study the Bible for yourself, it's helpful to "understand the language." There are some important words in the pages of scripture that may be unfamiliar, as well as some terms that don't appear in the Bible but summarize key biblical truths. Following is a list of these "theological" words that you'll want to know as you pursue a deeper understanding of God's Word. . .and God Himself.

1. **Adoption**: Adoption is when someone legally becomes a full member of a family that is not theirs by birth. In the New Testament, it refers to God's act of making us His children when we believe in Jesus and receive His Holy Spirit (John 1:12–13; Romans 8:15; Ephesians 1:5–6).

2. **Altar**: An altar is a structure on which sacrifices are made. In the Old Testament, people often set up altars for sacrifices to false gods. But there was one altar in the tabernacle, and later in the temple, that was dedicated to the worship of the one true God of Israel.

3. **Angel**: Angels are spiritual beings God created. Their primary role is to serve God, often as His messengers to humans. The Bible identifies two angels by name: Michael (Jude 9) and Gabriel (Luke 1:19).

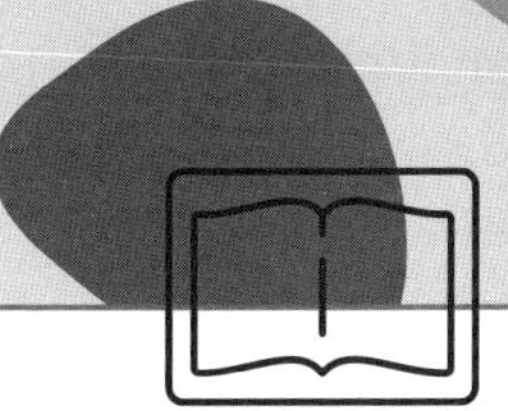

# Ten Biblical Names for God's Word

- Word of God (Luke 11:28)
- Word of Life (Philippians 2:16)
- Word of Christ (Colossians 3:16)
- The Book (Psalm 40:7)
- Book of the Law (Deuteronomy 31:26)
- Holy Scriptures (Romans 1:2)
- Living Words (Acts 7:38)
- Scriptures (John 5:39)
- Sword of the Spirit (Ephesians 6:17)
- Good Word of God (Hebrews 6:5)

4. **Anointing**: To anoint someone is to put oil on their head. In Old Testament times, anointing was done in special rituals to mark someone's appointment to an office such as high priest (Leviticus 16:32) or king (1 Samuel 9:16). It was a symbol of the presence of God being poured out on a person. In the New Testament, anointing is used when praying for someone's healing (James 5:14).
5. **Antichrist**: An antichrist is someone who stands against Jesus and denies that Jesus is the Christ, or Messiah (1 John 2:22). Some experts believe that "the man of sin" predicted in 2 Thessalonians 2:3–4 is the same as "the antichrist" in 1 John 2:18.
6. **Ark of the Covenant**: The ark of the covenant was a gold-covered wooden chest described in Exodus 25:10–22. The chest had a solid gold lid, called the atonement cover or mercy seat. On top were statues of two golden cherubim (angelic creatures) bowing down in worship. The ark represented the holy presence of God, so it could not be touched by human hands. Instead, poles were inserted through rings on the sides to carry the ark.
7. **Ascension**: The term refers to the moment when Jesus returned to heaven forty days after He rose from the dead (Luke 24:50–51; Acts 1:9–11). According to the Bible, Jesus now sits at the right hand of the Father (Hebrews 1:3), reigning with Him (Ephesians 1:19–21).

8. **Atonement**: Atonement brings together two individuals who have been separated because of sin. It refers to the work of Christ in taking our sin on Himself and dying to pay the penalty in our place. Forgiveness for our sins is possible through personally accepting, by faith, Christ's atoning sacrifice.

9. **Baptism**: The term literally means to dip, wash, immerse, submerge, or overwhelm. Baptism first appears in the New Testament when a prophet called John the Baptist baptized people in the Jordan River (Matthew 3:4–6). Christians are expected to be baptized as a sign of their repentance and new life in Jesus.

10. **Beatitudes**: The beatitudes are a series of blessings Jesus spoke in His Sermon on the Mount (Matthew 5:1–12). Jesus called His followers to certain attitudes and behaviors, promising good things to those who demonstrated His own nature.

11. **Begotten**: This word describes the special relationship between God the Father and Jesus the Son. Though God is the heavenly Father to many people who believe in Jesus, Jesus was God's "only begotten Son" (John 3:16).

12. **Blessed**: People are blessed when they have received the benefits of God's goodness in their lives. Blessed is also used twice in 1 Timothy to describe God Himself (1:11; 6:15).

13. **Born Again**: Jesus once told a Jewish religious leader named Nicodemus that in order to see

the kingdom of God, one must be "born again" (John 3:3), or born from above. This is not a physical rebirth but a spiritual one (John 3:8). It happens when a person repents of sin and trusts in Jesus as Savior (John 3:16).

14. **Canon**: The "canon of scripture" is the accepted list of the sixty-six Bible books. The process of compiling the books of the Bible did not happen all at once. The Old Testament canon was finalized before the start of the first century BC (before Christ) by Jewish religious leaders. The New Testament was completed many years after the death of the apostles. Early churches had recognized many of the New Testament books from the time they were first written, but near the end of the fourth century AD ("anno Domini," or after the birth of Jesus), church leaders agreed upon the final list.

15. **Creation**: The word refers to God's act of making all things—the universe, the earth, and all living creatures—out of nothing (Genesis 1–2). God simply spoke most things into existence, though He personally fashioned the first man and woman. He called His finished creation "very good" (Genesis 1:31).

16. **Disciple**: A disciple is a person who learns from a teacher. A disciple of Jesus Christ is someone who follows Him, learns from Him, and obeys His teaching. Jesus issued a final command to His disciples to go out to the nations and "make disciples"

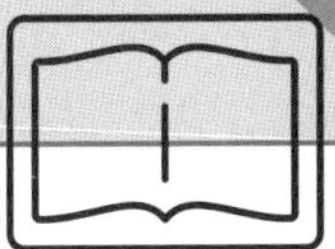

# The Beatitudes

"Blessed are the poor in spirit,
for theirs is the kingdom of heaven."

(Matthew 5:3)

"Blessed are those who mourn,
for they shall be comforted."

(Matthew 5:4)

"Blessed are the meek,
for they shall inherit the earth."

(Matthew 5:5)

"Blessed are those who hunger and thirst
after righteousness, for they shall be filled."

(Matthew 5:6)

"Blessed are the merciful,
for they shall obtain mercy."

(Matthew 5:7)

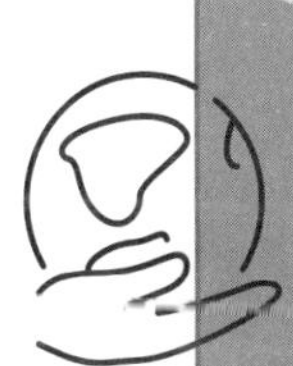

"Blessed are the pure in heart,
for they shall see God."

(Matthew 5:8)

"Blessed are the peacemakers, for they
shall be called the children of God."

(Matthew 5:9)

"Blessed are those who are persecuted
for righteousness' sake, for theirs
is the kingdom of heaven."

(Matthew 5:10)

(Matthew 28:19 NIV). All Christians are called to be disciples of Jesus.

17. **Doctrine**: The word literally means "teaching." In the Bible, doctrine is teaching on a particular subject. The Trinity, creation, sin, and salvation are all examples of doctrine taught in the Bible.

18. **Epistle**: An epistle is a New Testament letter written by an apostle to a church or an individual. Paul wrote Romans, 1–2 Corinthians, Galatians, Ephesians, Philippians, Colossians, and 1–2 Thessalonians to churches of various cities or regions. He also wrote 1–2 Timothy, Titus, and Philemon to individuals. James, 1–2 Peter, 1–3 John, and Jude are epistles by the author whose name they bear. The writer of the epistle to the Hebrews isn't known for certain.

19. **Exile**: Exile is the forced removal from one's home country. In the Old Testament, the northern kingdom of Israel was invaded by the armies of Assyria, and many of its people were carried off to other lands (1 Chronicles 5:26; 2 Kings 15:29). Later, the southern kingdom of Judah was attacked and conquered by the armies of Babylon. Many of those who lived through the invasion were carried off into captivity within the Babylonian Empire.

20. **Exodus**: This word means "departure." The book of Exodus got its title for telling how God, using a humble man named Moses, delivered

the people of Israel from captivity and slavery in Egypt. This event is remembered every year in the Jewish Passover celebration.

21. **Fall**: The phrase "the fall" refers to events that took place in Genesis 3. It recounts how the first human beings, Adam and Eve, chose sin over obedience to God. When they disobeyed, they lost His blessing and received a curse. Adam and Eve suffered terrible consequences for their sin, as have all their descendants—every human being throughout history.

22. **Gentile**: The word refers to anyone who is not Jewish. The Bible teaches that the people of Israel were the ones God chose to bring the Messiah—Jesus Christ—into the world. But scripture also clearly states that Jesus is the Savior for all people groups, Jews and Gentiles alike.

23. **Gospel**: "The gospel" is the good news of salvation through Jesus—as in "Go into all the world and preach the gospel" (Mark 16:15). This is the message Jesus brought to earth, the same message the apostles Paul, Peter, and John faithfully preached after Jesus returned to heaven. It is summed up in John 3:16 (NLV): "For God so loved the world that He gave His only Son. Whoever puts his trust in God's Son will not be lost but will have life that lasts forever." The term *Gospel* also refers to the four Bible accounts

of Jesus' life, death, and resurrection: Matthew, Mark, Luke, and John.

24. **Grace**: This is God's goodness and blessing, freely given to people who do not deserve it. Human beings cannot be saved by any good things we do. It is only through God's act of grace in sending His Son, Jesus Christ, to pay the price of our sins on the cross that we can live forever in His presence.

25. **Great Commission**: Before He returned to heaven, Jesus spoke what is called "the Great Commission": "All power has been given to Me in heaven and on earth. Go and make followers of all the nations. Baptize them in the name of the Father and of the Son and of the Holy Spirit. Teach them to do all the things I have told you. And I am with you always, even to the end of the world" (Matthew 28:18–20 NLV). All Christians are expected to proclaim the gospel message.

26. **Heaven**: Heaven is the place where God dwells in all His glory. It is the place where Jesus lived before becoming a man and where He returned after His death, burial, and resurrection. Now heaven is where Jesus sits at the right hand of the Father, ruling over all things (Hebrews 1:3; 1 Peter 3:22). Angels and other heavenly beings live in heaven, worshipping and serving God (Isaiah 6:1–3; Job 1:6; Luke 1:19). It is also the eternal home of those who have trusted Jesus for their salvation.

27. **Hell**: Hell is the final destination for people who do not trust in Jesus Christ for their salvation. It is a place of eternal punishment for Satan and his demons (Revelation 20:10), along with human beings who reject Christ (Hebrews 10:26–27). In the *Gospels*, Jesus spoke often of hell, telling His listeners that whoever refuses to repent of sin will suffer there for eternity (Mark 9:43–48).

28. **Incarnation**: The doctrine of the incarnation explains that God became flesh when Jesus Christ came into the world as a baby. The Bible says that Jesus is fully God and fully man, which is demonstrated by the fact that Jesus was conceived through the Holy Spirit, not a human father (Luke 1:35). Jesus was called Immanuel, meaning "God with us" (Matthew 1:23).

29. **Intercession**: The word means asking God for something on behalf of another person. In the Old Testament, it was the priests' job to intercede with God on behalf of the people. The New Testament teaches that Jesus intercedes to His Father for His people (Hebrews 7:23–25; Romans 8:34). The Bible also says that we as Christians should intercede for all people, especially those in positions of authority (1 Timothy 2:1–3).

30. **Israel and Judah**: Judah in the south and Israel in the north are the two kingdoms that emerged after the united kingdom of Israel divided upon King Solomon's death. The capital city of Judah was Jerusalem, while Israel's

capital was Samaria. Because of their sin, both kingdoms were conquered by other world powers.

31. **Justification**: In the Bible, the word describes God making sinners right with Him. No one can be righteous based on his own efforts. People need God to cleanse and forgive their sin to be received into His family. Jesus' death on the cross paid for human sin; when we trust in Him for justification, by simple faith, we are cleansed and made right.

32. **Law of Moses**: Also known as the Mosaic Law or simply "the law," these are the collected laws and rules God gave the Israelites through Moses. They are found in the first five books of the Hebrew Bible, called the Torah. They were intended to guide the Israelites in living lives that pleased God.

33. **Omnipotence**: This term describes God's all-powerful nature. Nothing is impossible for Him (John 13:3; Ephesians 1:18–23; Matthew 19:26). Only God is omnipotent, which is an excellent reason to trust Him completely.

34. **Omnipresence**: This means that God is not confined by time and space like people are, so there is no place in the universe where He is not present. Nobody can hide from God or think He's unaware of their actions. On the positive side, we can always know that we are never out of God's reach (Psalm 139; Jeremiah 23:23–24).

35. **Omniscience**: This means that God is all-knowing (Job 37:16; John 16:30; 1 John 3:20). He knows everything in the universe, including the past, the present, and the eternal future. And God knows everything about every human who has ever lived.

36. **Original Sin**: The doctrine of original sin (found in Romans 5:12–21) is the teaching that every human being is affected by the disobedience of Adam and Eve (Genesis 3). Every one of us has inherited a sinful nature and share in Adam and Eve's guilt. People are born sinful (Psalm 51:5; Proverbs 20:9), incapable of pleasing God by their own actions (Romans 8:8). To be right with God and escape judgment, we must have faith in God and His saving grace, which is found in Jesus Christ.

37. **Pentecost**: This is the Greek name for the Jewish Festival of Weeks, which celebrates God's provision for His people. They were expected to give the firstfruits of their harvest back to God (Exodus 34:22; Deuteronomy 16:9–12). Pentecost takes place seven weeks after Passover. Acts 2 marks Pentecost as the day the Holy Spirit came to live in followers of Jesus. They were "filled with the Holy Spirit" (Acts 2:4) and were empowered to share the good news of Jesus with the crowds. Peter declared this event to be the fulfillment of God's promise to pour out His Spirit in the last days (Joel 2:28–32).

38. **Prophet**: Prophets were God's chosen instruments to speak His words to other people. In the Old Testament, God chose many men as prophets—people like Moses, Samuel, Elijah, Elisha, Isaiah, and Jeremiah. Many of them wrote books of prophecy that became part of the Old Testament.

39. **Rapture**: You won't find this word anywhere in the Bible, but the idea is in 1 Thessalonians 4:16–17, where living believers at the time of Jesus' Second Coming are "caught up together. . .in the clouds." When Jesus returns in glory, the dead in Christ are raised first, just before the living Christians are lifted up from the earth.

### Words You Won't Find in the Bible

Though the words *Trinity*, *rapture*, and *evangelism* are commonly used in Christian circles, they don't appear anywhere in the Bible.

40. **Redemption**: The word indicates a buying back or ransom of people who've been enslaved, followed by setting them free. In the Old Testament, God's great act of redemption was freeing the Israelites from their slavery in Egypt (Exodus 6:6; 20:1–2). In the New Testament, God's act of redemption is setting all His people free from slavery to sin. He accomplished this through

the death and resurrection of Jesus Christ (Galatians 4:3–5).

41. **Repent**: The word means to change your mind and turn back to God. Repentance begins with being sorry for your sin, confessing to God that you've been going in the wrong direction, and then changing your life so that you're living His way (2 Corinthians 7:10). Repentance is necessary in order for human beings to be saved (Acts 2:37–41; 3:19).

42. **Resurrection**: The raising to life of someone who has died physically. Jesus stated several times that He had power over death (Matthew 16:21; John 5:24; 10:17–18), to the extent that He claimed to be "the resurrection and the life" (John 11:25). Jesus raised people from the dead during His ministry on earth, but His power over death was most notably displayed in His own resurrection.

43. **Righteousness**: This means being in right standing with God, living in a way that pleases Him. The Bible teaches that only God is truly righteous; all people fall short of His standards (Romans 3:10, 23; 1 John 2:1). No matter how hard we try, our own efforts can never make us righteous (Romans 3:20). God dealt with this problem by sending Jesus to die on the cross, taking our unrighteousness on Himself and suffering God's wrath for it (Romans 3:24–26; 1 Peter 3:18).

44. **Sacrifice**: In Old Testament times, God set up

a system of sacrifices so people could receive forgiveness for sin. Animals that were sacrificed bore God's wrath instead of the people themselves. But these sacrifices foreshadowed the one great sacrifice to come: Jesus' death on the cross for the sins of the world.

45. **Sanctification**: This theological word describes how we as humans can be made holy. Sanctification is necessary for enjoying a relationship with a holy God who cannot bear the presence of sin. Sanctification (which requires our effort) follows justification (which is purely God's work through our faith). Sanctification comes through the internal workings of the Holy Spirit in our lives.

46. **Scripture**: The word is used in the Bible to refer to itself (Matthew 21:42). The scriptures are the collection of writings—what we call the Bible—that reveal God's truth to us. As the divine author of scripture, the Holy Spirit inspired human authors to write down God's words (2 Timothy 3:16–17; 2 Peter 1:21). All scripture points to Jesus Christ and His mission to rescue humanity from its own sinfulness, bringing people back into relationship with God (Luke 24:27).

47. **Second Coming**: This term refers to the future physical return of Jesus Christ to the earth. The Bible teaches that Jesus will return suddenly (1 Thessalonians 5:2), in the sight of all people (Revelation 1:7). He will return in His glory (Matthew 16:27), judging the world

(Acts 17:31) and ushering in the new creation (2 Peter 3:13). The Bible teaches that we can't know the time of Jesus' return, so we must live in perpetual readiness.

48. **Tabernacle**: The tabernacle was a large portable tent surrounded by a courtyard. It was a place where God would dwell while His people were in the wilderness, and even in the Promised Land before the temple was constructed in Jerusalem. Moses met with God at the tabernacle, and priests offered sacrifices to atone for the people's sins. In Exodus 25–27, God gave Moses very specific instructions for building the tabernacle.

49. **Temple**: The temple was a magnificent building in Jerusalem where God's presence dwelt and where the people could worship Him. It was built under the leadership of King Solomon and stood for four centuries until it was destroyed by the Babylonians around 587 BC (1 Kings 5–8; 2 Chronicles 36:15–23). A second temple was later rebuilt on the same site.

50. **Trinity**: This term doesn't appear in scripture, but the Bible is clear that God has eternally existed as one God in three distinct persons—Father, Son, and Holy Spirit. Members of the Trinity are indicated throughout the Bible, from Genesis 1 to Revelation 22, and mentioned together in passages like Matthew 3:16–17, where the Father, Son, and Holy Spirit are all present at Jesus' baptism.

# 25 Great Promises in the Bible

From Genesis 1 to the last few words of Revelation, the Bible is filled with God's promises—by some counts, around 1,260 of them. And God always, without fail, keeps His promises. That's what He meant when He said, "None of my words will be delayed any longer; whatever I say will be fulfilled" (Ezekiel 12:28 NIV).

Here are several amazing promises from scripture, all of which apply to *you* as His beloved daughter:

1. **Abundant Life in Christ**: "The robber comes only to steal and to kill and to destroy. I came so they might have life, a great full life" (John 10:10 NLV). / *Also see John 14:19; Romans 6:8, 11; Ephesians 2:1, 5–6; 1 John 5:12*

2. **Adoption into God's Family Through Jesus**: "All those who are led by the Holy Spirit are sons of God. You should not act like people who are owned by someone. They are always afraid. Instead, the Holy Spirit makes us His sons, and we can call to Him, 'My Father'" (Romans 8:14–15 NLV). / *Also see Romans 9:26; 2 Corinthians 6:18; Galatians 4:4–7; 1 John 3:1–2*

3. **Jesus Prays for Us**: "And so Jesus is able, now and forever, to save from the punishment

of sin all who come to God through Him because He lives forever to pray for them" (Hebrews 7:25 NLV). / *Also see Romans 8:34*

4. **Christ's Return**: "For the Lord Himself will come down from heaven with a loud call. The head angel will speak with a loud voice. God's horn will give its sounds. First, those who belong to Christ will come out of their graves to meet the Lord. Then, those of us who are still living here on earth will be gathered together with them in the clouds. We will meet the Lord in the sky and be with Him forever" (1 Thessalonians 4:16–17 NLV). / *Also see Matthew 24:30; Mark 14:62; John 14:3; 1 Corinthians 4:5; 2 Timothy 4:8; Revelation 1:7*

5. **Confident Access to God**: "Christian brothers, now we know we can go into the Holiest Place of All because the blood of Jesus was given. We now come to God by the new and living way. Christ made this way for us. He opened the curtain, which was His own body" (Hebrews 10:19–20 NLV). / *Also see Ephesians 2:18; 3:12; 1 John 5:14–16*

6. **God Provides Deliverance in Times of Trouble**: "A man who does what is right and good may have many troubles. But the Lord takes him out of them all" (Psalm 34:19 NLV). / *Also see Job 8:20–21; Psalm 18:27–28; 42:11; 71:20*

7. **Eternal Life with God in Heaven**: "There are many rooms in My Father's house. If it were

not so, I would have told you. I am going away to make a place for you. After I go and make a place for you, I will come back and take you with Me. Then you may be where I am" (John 14:2–3 NLV). / *Also see Romans 2:7; 1 Corinthians 2:9; Hebrews 4:9; 1 Peter 1:9; 2 Peter 3:13; Revelation 3:4*

8. **Forgiveness of Sin**: "If we tell Him our sins, He is faithful and we can depend on Him to forgive us of our sins. He will make our lives clean from all sin" (1 John 1:9 NLV). / *Also see Psalm 65:3; 103:9–12; Isaiah 43:25; 44:22; Micah 7:18–19; Matthew 26:28; Ephesians 1:7; Hebrews 10:17; Revelation 1:5*

9. **God Hears Our Prayers**: "Ask, and what you are asking for will be given to you. Look, and what you are looking for you will find. Knock, and the door you are knocking on will be opened to you. Everyone who asks receives what he asks for. Everyone who looks finds what he is looking for. Everyone who knocks has the door opened to him" (Matthew 7:7–8 NLV). / *Also see Psalm 4:3; 50:15; Proverbs 15:29; Matthew 21:22; James 5:15–16*

10. **God's Enduring Love**: "The Lord came to us from far away, saying, 'I have loved you with a love that lasts forever. So I have helped you come to Me with loving-kindness'" (Jeremiah 31:3 NLV). / *Also Zephaniah 3:17; John 16:27; Ephesians 2:4; 2 Thessalonians 2:16*

11. **God's Gift of His Spirit**: "You are sinful and you know how to give good things to your children. How much more will your Father in heaven give the Holy Spirit to those who ask Him?" (Luke 11:13 NLV). / *Also see Proverbs 1:23; Isaiah 32:15; John 14:16–18; Galatians 3:14; 2 Timothy 1:14*

12. **God's Mercy**: "For the Lord your God is a God of loving-pity. He will not leave you or destroy you or forget the agreement He promised to your fathers" (Deuteronomy 4:31 NLV). / *Also see Exodus 33:19; Psalm 103:13; Isaiah 30:18, 48:9*

13. **God Will Never Abandon You**: "But Zion said, 'The Lord has left me alone. The Lord has forgotten me.' 'Can a woman forget her nursing child? Can she have no pity on the son to whom she gave birth? Even these may forget, but I will not forget you. See, I have marked your names on My hands. Your walls are always before Me'" (Isaiah 49:14–16 NLV). / *Also see Psalm 9:10; 94:14; Isaiah 54:9–10; Jeremiah 32:40; Hebrews 13:5*

14. **Guidance from Above**: "The Lord will always lead you. He will meet the needs of your soul in the dry times and give strength to your body. You will be like a garden that has enough water, like a well of water

that never dries up" (Isaiah 58:11 NLV). / *Also see Deuteronomy 32:10–12; Psalm 23:2–3; 73:24; Isaiah 30:21*

15. **Help in Overcoming Temptation**: "You have never been tempted to sin in any different way than other people. God is faithful. He will not allow you to be tempted more than you can take. But when you are tempted, He will make a way for you to keep from falling into sin" (1 Corinthians 10:13 NLV). / *Also see Romans 8:37; 2 Corinthians 12:9; Hebrews 2:18; 2 Peter 2:9; 1 John 4:4*

16. **Justification Through Jesus Christ**: "Anyone can be made right with God by the free gift of His loving-favor. It is Jesus Christ Who bought them with His blood and made them free from their sins" (Romans 3:24 NLV). / *Also see Acts 13:39; 2 Corinthians 5:21*

17. **No Condemnation**: "Now, because of this, those who belong to Christ will not suffer the punishment of sin" (Romans 8:1 NLV). / *Also see Romans 8:33–34*

18. **Peace from God**: "Do not worry. Learn to pray about everything. Give thanks to God as you ask Him for what you need. The peace of God is much greater than the human mind can understand. This peace will keep your hearts and minds through Christ Jesus" (Philippians 4:6–7 NLV). / *Also see Leviticus 26:6; Psalm 29:11; 119:165; Isaiah 26:12*

19. **Power from God to Persevere**: "I give them life that lasts forever. They will never be punished. No one is able to take them out of My hand. My Father Who gave them to Me is greater than all. No one is able to take them out of My Father's hand" (John 10:28–29 NLV). / *Also see Romans 8:38–39; 1 Corinthians 1:8; Philippians 1:6; 1 Thessalonians 5:23–24; 2 Thessalonians 3:3*

20. **Provision from God**: "First of all, look for the holy nation of God. Be right with Him. All these other things will be given to you also" (Matthew 6:33 NLV). / *Also see Psalm 23:1; 37:3; Matthew 6:26; Philippians 4:19; 1 Timothy 6:6, 17*

21. **Reconciled to God Through Christ**: "Now that we have been saved from the punishment of sin by the blood of Christ, He will save us from God's anger also. We hated God. But we were saved from the punishment of sin by the death of Christ. He has brought us back to God and we will be saved by His life" (Romans 5:9–10 NLV). *Also see 2 Corinthians 5:18–19; Ephesians 2:13–17; Colossians 1:21–23; Hebrews 2:17*

22. **Rewards for Seeking God**: "A man cannot please God unless he has faith. Anyone who comes to God must believe that He is. That one must also know that God gives what is promised to the one who keeps on looking for Him" (Hebrews 11:6 NLV). / *Also see 1 Chronicles 28:9; 2 Chronicles 15:2; Psalm 9:10;*

*Jeremiah 29:13; Amos 5:4; Acts 17:27*

23. **Victory over the Devil**: "I have written to you, fathers, because you know Him Who has been from the beginning. I have written to you, young men, because you are strong. You have kept God's Word in your hearts. You have power over the devil" (1 John 2:14 NLV). / *Also see Romans 16:20; James 4:7; 1 John 5:18*

24. **Victory over the World**: "But take hope! I have power over the world!" (John 16:33 NLV). / *Also see John 17:15; Galatians 1:4; 6:14; 1 John 5:4–5*

25. **God Keeps All His Promises**: "Know then that the Lord your God is God, the faithful God. He keeps His promise and shows His loving-kindness to those who love Him and keep His Laws, even to a thousand family groups in the future" (Deuteronomy 7:9 NLV). / *Also see Numbers 23:19; Psalm 89:34; Isaiah 46:11; Romans 4:21; 2 Timothy 2:13; Hebrews 6:18*

# 25 Important Titles of Jesus

1. **Advocate** (1 John 2:1)
2. **Alpha and Omega** (Revelation 1:8)

3. **Author and Finisher of Our Faith** (Hebrews 12:2)
4. **Bread of Life** (John 6:35)
5. **Chief Shepherd** (1 Peter 5:4)
6. **The Christ** (1 John 2:22)
7. **Faithful and True Witness** (Revelation 3:14)
8. **God** (John 1:1; Hebrews 1:8; Romans 9:5)
9. **Great High Priest** (Hebrews 4:14)
10. **Horn of Salvation** (Luke 1:69)
11. **I Am** (John 8:58)
12. **King of Kings and Lord of Lords** (Revelation 19:16)
13. **Lamb of God** (John 1:29)
14. **Last Adam** (1 Corinthians 15:45)
15. **Light of the World** (John 8:12)
16. **Lion of the Tribe of Judah** (Revelation 5:5)
17. **Mediator** (1 Timothy 2:5)
18. **Messiah** (Daniel 9:25–26)
19. **Mighty God** (Isaiah 9:6)
20. **Redeemer** (Isaiah 54:5)
21. **Resurrection and Life** (John 11:25)
22. **Savior** (Ephesians 5:23; 2 Peter 2:20)
23. **Son of God** (John 1:49)
24. **Wonderful Counselor** (Isaiah 9:6)
25. **The Word** (John 1:1)

2

# The BIBLE'S Important PEOPLE and PLACES

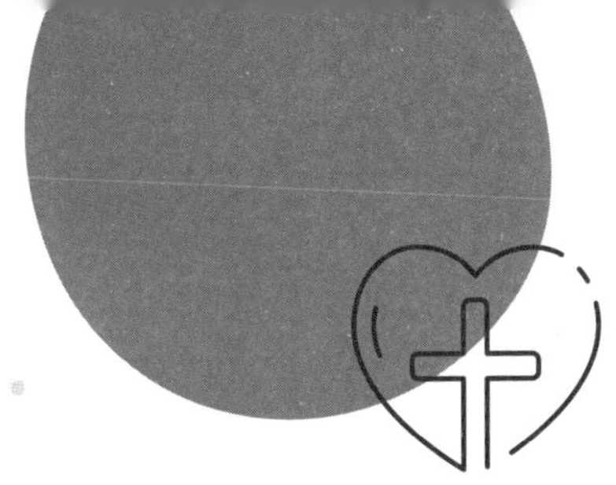

The Bible includes many stories of God's interactions with humanity. These were real people who lived in real places.

Knowing something of these important people and places can aid your understanding as you read the Bible. God included these details in His written Word to teach us important lessons about His love, His holiness, and His plan for humankind.

# Fifty of the Bible's Most Important People

1. **Aaron**: Older brother of Moses, he was called into God's service when Moses hesitated to confront Pharaoh over his enslavement of the Israelites. He was God's spokesman in support of Moses' leadership for nearly forty years, the first priest of Israel, and the head of a family line of priests that continued for more than a thousand years.

2. **Abraham**: The new name for Abram, the man God called out of Ur of the Chaldees and into the Promised Land. This new name was a

symbol of the covenant between God and Abraham. The Lord promised to build a nation through Abraham and his wife Sarai (who God renamed Sarah), though she was too old to have children. In time, God gave Sarah and Abraham a miracle son named Isaac, a patriarch of Israel, the nation God promised.

3. **Adam**: The first man, created by God to have dominion over the earth. Adam's first act was to name the animals; then God created Adam's wife, Eve, as "a helper that is right for him" (Genesis 2:18 NLV). God gave the first couple the beautiful Garden of Eden to care for. There Satan, in the form of a serpent, tempted Eve. God had warned them not to eat the fruit of the tree of the knowledge of good and evil, but Eve gave in to temptation and then offered the fruit to Adam, who also ate.

4. **Barnabas**: A Christian from Cyprus who sold land and gave the profit to the church. After Saul's conversion, Barnabas introduced this former persecutor of the church to the apostles and spoke up for him. Saul and Barnabas went on a missionary journey together.

5. **Cyrus**: King of Persia who commanded that the temple in Jerusalem be rebuilt. He ordered all his people to give donations to help the Jews, and he returned the temple vessels that Nebuchadnezzar of Babylon had taken.

6. **Daniel**: A major prophet of the Old Testament. As a child, Daniel was taken into exile in Babylon. Because he refused to defile himself with meat and wine from the king's table, God blessed him with knowledge and wisdom. Daniel interpreted two dreams for King Nebuchadnezzar, who made him ruler over the province of Babylon. During King Belshazzar's reign, Daniel interpreted the meaning of the mysterious handwriting on the wall. For this he was made third ruler in the kingdom.

7. **David**: Israel's second and greatest king. As a young shepherd and musician, David was anointed king by the prophet Samuel in the disobedient King Saul's place. David gained national prominence by killing the Philistine giant Goliath. Following a battle with the Philistines and the deaths of Saul and his sons, David was anointed king of Judah. Later, he became king of all Israel. David wrote many of the psalms. Though he was a great king, he was still a flawed man who made some terrible mistakes.

8. **Elijah**: An Old Testament prophet for the northern kingdom of Israel. His prophecy that no rain would fall, except at his command, angered the wicked King Ahab, and Elijah had to flee across the Jordan River to a place called Zarephath. God hid him for three years, then sent him to Mount Carmel. There, Elijah had a showdown with the priests of Baal that proved the Lord was God.

9. **Elisabeth**: Wife of the priest Zacharias and mother of John the Baptist. Elisabeth had been unable to have a baby, but her husband received a vision promising that she would conceive. When Elisabeth heard this, she rejoiced at God's favor. Her cousin Mary, the mother of Jesus, visited her for three months after Mary learned she would bear Jesus, the Messiah.

10. **Elisha**: The prophet Elijah's successor and disciple. Elisha saw Elijah carried up to heaven on a whirlwind of fire and received a double portion of his spirit. Elisha performed many miracles. At his command, Naaman, a Syrian captain, bathed in the Jordan and was healed of leprosy.

11. **Esther**: The Jewish wife of the Persian king Ahasuerus. Angered by his first wife, Vashti, Ahasuerus sought a new bride from among the women of his kingdom. He married the beautiful Esther and made her his queen. When the king's counselor Haman plotted to kill the Jewish people, Esther revealed her ethnicity and requested his help. Ahasuerus sided with Esther, killing Haman and allowing the Jews to defend themselves.

12. **Eve**: Adam's wife, "the mother of all living" (Genesis 3:20 NLV). Tempted by the serpent, Eve ate fruit from the tree of the knowledge

of good and evil and offered some to her husband, who also ate. Suddenly fearful of God because of their sin, they hid from Him. God said Adam and Eve would die, but also hinted at the saving work of Jesus Christ (Genesis 3:15).

13. **Ezra**: An Israelite scribe and teacher of the law who returned from the Babylonian Exile along with some priests, Levites, temple servants, and others. Ezra had the backing of King Artaxerxes of Persia and returned with money and the temple vessels. Ezra prayed for his people, read them the law, and called on them to confess their sin.

14. **Gideon**: The fifth judge of Israel, whom God raised up to lead his nation against the Midianites. The angel of the Lord appeared to Gideon when he was hiding his threshing from the enemy, told him God was with him, and called him a "powerful soldier" (Judges 6:12 NLV). He is known for testing the Lord's will with a fleece.

15. **Hannah**: Hannah could not bear a child. Her husband, Elkanah, loved her, though his second wife abused her. Distraught, Hannah prayed at the tabernacle, promising God that if He gave her a child, she would return the boy to His service. In time, Hannah conceived and bore Samuel, who became a powerful prophet of Israel.

16. **Hezekiah**: The thirteenth ruler of Judah who did right in God's eyes. Hezekiah removed pagan worship from the kingdom and kept God's commandments. Under his command, the Levites cleansed the temple and restored worship. He is considered Judah's greatest king.

17. **Hosea**: A minor prophet whom God commanded to marry an immoral, unfaithful woman named Gomer. She ran away with another man, but God told Hosea to go and win her back. The prophet's chaotic life paralleled the unfaithfulness of the people of Israel, who had abandoned their covenant with the God who still loved them.

18. **Isaac**: The son of Abraham and Sarah whom God promised to the long-barren couple. God tested Abraham by commanding him to sacrifice Isaac at Moriah. There, Abraham built an altar and placed his son atop it. But the angel of the Lord stopped the sacrifice, and God provided a ram instead. Isaac later married a woman named Rebekah. When she struggled to conceive, Isaac prayed for a child. She bore the twins Esau and Jacob.

19. **Isaiah**: A prophet of Jerusalem who served under kings Uzziah, Jotham, Ahaz, and Hezekiah. This aristocratic prophet was married to a prophetess and had at least two children. Isaiah warned Ahaz of an attack by Syria and warned against making treaties with

# Bible People Whose Names Were Changed

- Abram to Abraham (Genesis 17:5)
- Sarai to Sarah (Genesis 17:15)
- Jacob to Israel (Genesis 32:28; 35:10)
- Simon to Peter (translation of "Cephas") (John 1:42)
- Saul of Tarsus to Paul (Acts 13:9)
- Daniel to Belteshazzar (Daniel 1:6–7)
- Hananiah to Shadrach (Daniel 1:6–7)
- Mishael to Meshach (Daniel 1:6–7)
- Azariah to Abed-nego (Daniel 1:6–7)

foreign nations. His long prophecy is sometimes called "the fifth Gospel" for its heavy emphasis on the life of the Messiah, Jesus.

20. **Jacob**: Isaac and Rebekah's son, born clinging to the heel of his twin brother, Esau. As a young man, when the hungry Esau returned from hunting and asked Jacob for his stew, Jacob sold some to him for his valuable birthright. Later, tricked by his uncle Laban, Jacob married both of his daughters, Leah and Rachel. From them and their handmaids, Jacob had twelve sons, leaders of the twelve tribes of Israel, the nation called by a new name God gave Jacob (Genesis 35:10).

21. **James**: Jesus' half brother, called James the Less (or Younger). James became a leader in the early church at Jerusalem. Paul visited him after returning from Arabia. When James saw that Paul had received God's grace, he and the other leaders accepted him for ministry. This James is believed by many to be the writer of the New Testament book of James.

22. **Jeremiah**: A prophet of Judah during the reigns of kings Josiah, Jehoahaz, Jehoiakim, Jehoiachin, and Zedekiah. Following Assyria's destruction of Israel, Babylon threatened

Judah. The turmoil of his age was clearly reflected in Jeremiah's gloomy prophecies. He condemned Judah for idolatry and called the nation to repent. God warned of Judah's destruction and Jeremiah mourned over it, yet Jerusalem refused to change. Jeremiah's book of Lamentations mourns the consequences.

23. **Jesus**: Humanity's Savior. As the Son of God, Jesus has always existed as one member of the Trinity. Through the Holy Spirit He was incarnated in the womb of Mary and born in a Bethlehem stable. He grew up in Nazareth and began His ministry around age thirty. Jesus died on a Roman cross to take the punishment of humanity's sin. After His resurrection, He appeared first to Mary Magdalene and then to other followers. He commissioned believers to spread the good news and ascended to heaven after forty days

24. **Job**: A righteous man from the land of Uz. Satan argued that Job was faithful to God only because of his many physical blessings. For a time, God gave Job into Satan's power, and Job suffered terribly, losing his wealth, his health, and even his children. Yet he remained faithful. In the end, God restored Job's physical possessions and gave him ten more children.

25. **John**: A son of Zebedee and brother of James, John became Jesus' disciple when He called

the brothers to leave their fishing boat and follow Him. In his Gospel, John called himself "the disciple Jesus loved." Part of Jesus' inner circle, John—along with James and Peter—witnessed events such as the healing of Jairus' daughter and the transfiguration. John also wrote three letters that bear his name and the book of Revelation.

26. **John the Baptist**: John was a relative of Jesus, born to the elderly couple Zacharias and Elisabeth. Before Jesus began His ministry, John preached a message of repentance in the desert. Those who confessed their sins were baptized in the Jordan River. John reluctantly baptized Jesus, who had no sin to confess but said the ceremony would fulfill all righteousness (Matthew 3:15). He was beheaded after confronting King Herod about his adultery.

27. **Jonah**: An Old Testament minor prophet whom God commanded to preach in Nineveh, the capital of Israel's enemy Assyria. Fearing that God would show mercy to them, Jonah fled on a ship headed in the opposite direction. When a violent storm struck, sailors tossed Jonah overboard at his request. Jonah was swallowed by a fish and miraculously kept alive for three days. When he praised God, the fish vomited him onto land and Jonah obeyed God. The people listened and repented.

28. **Joseph, the patriarch**: Son of Jacob and Rachel. He was Jacob's favorite son, which

made his ten older brothers jealous. When Joseph told them he'd dreamed he would one day rule over them, they threw him into an empty pit, then sold him to passing traders. Carried to Egypt, Joseph became slave to the captain of Pharaoh's guard. Then he was incarcerated after rejecting the seduction of the captain's wife, who falsely accused him of impropriety. In prison, Joseph interpreted the dreams of two of Pharaoh's servants, then was asked to interpret Pharaoh's prophetic dream. Pharaoh, impressed, made Joseph second-in-command in Egypt, where his family was ultimately reunited.

29. **Joseph, Jesus' earthly father**: Husband of Mary and foster father of Jesus. A carpenter, Joseph was betrothed to Mary when she conceived Jesus through the Holy Spirit. He planned to divorce her quietly, but an angel told him to go ahead and marry her, as she would bear the Messiah. For a Roman census, Joseph traveled with Mary to Bethlehem, where Jesus was born.

30. **Joshua**: Moses' right-hand man. The son of Nun, Joshua led Israel to victory against the Amalekites. He spied out Canaan before the Israelites entered the land, and he came back with a positive report. For his faith, he was one of only two men of his generation who survived the wilderness wandering. God chose Joshua to succeed Moses as Israel's leader. After Moses' death, Joshua led the Israelites into the Promised Land.

31. **Judas Iscariot**: The disciple who betrayed Jesus. He was made one of the Twelve by Jesus and put in charge of the disciples' money, though he was secretly a thief (John 12:6). Judas went to the chief priests, offering to betray Jesus for thirty pieces of silver. At the Last Supper, Jesus predicted Judas' betrayal and even handed him a morsel of food to identify him as the betrayer. Following Jesus' death, in deep remorse, Judas returned the money to the priests and hanged himself.

32. **Luke**: Known as the "beloved physician," Luke was likely a Gentile believer who became a ministry companion of the apostle Paul. Writer of the third Gospel and the book of Acts, Luke was an excellent historian, as indicated by the careful detail in his accounts. The use of "we" in Acts 16:10 indicates that Luke had joined Paul and Silas on their missionary journey.

33. **Mary**: Jesus' mother, who as a young virgin received news from an angel that she would bear the Messiah. Mary traveled with her betrothed, Joseph, to Bethlehem, where Jesus was born. When she and Joseph brought Jesus to the temple, Mary heard Simeon's and Anna's prophecies about her son. She stood by the cross as Jesus died and was in the upper room with the disciples after His ascension.

34. **Matthew**: A tax collector, also called Levi, who left his vocation to follow Jesus. Although Matthew does not identify himself as the writer of the Gospel named for him, the early church ascribed the book to him.

35. **Moses**: The Old Testament prophet through whom God gave the people of Israel the law. Because Pharaoh commanded the killing of all male newborn Israelites, Moses' mother hid him in a basket in the Nile River. There he was found by an Egyptian princess, who raised him. As a young man, Moses killed an Egyptian for abusing an Israelite slave and fled to Midian, where he met God in a burning bush. The Lord sent Moses back to Egypt, where his brother Aaron became his spokesman. Moses confronted Pharaoh, telling him to let God's people go.

36. **Nebuchadnezzar**: This king of Babylon besieged Jerusalem twice and carried Judah's people into exile. He is the king who threw Shadrach, Meshach, and Abed-nego into the "fiery furnace" for refusing to bow to his golden statue. Nebuchadnezzar also lost his sanity for a period of time as punishment for his pride. When he regained his senses, he praised the one true God.

37. **Nehemiah**: A Jewish man who asked his boss, the Persian king Artaxerxes, for permission to return to war-ravaged Jerusalem. Nehemiah became governor of Judah. Under

his leadership, the people were able to rebuild Jerusalem's walls in a remarkably short time.

38. **Nicodemus**: A member of the Jewish ruling council—the Sanhedrin—who went to Jesus at night to learn more about Him. Jesus told Nicodemus that he needed to be born again. Later, when Jewish leaders wanted to arrest Jesus, Nicodemus stood up for Him. After Jesus' death, Nicodemus provided the myrrh and aloe mixture with which the body was prepared for burial.

39. **Noah**: The man God chose to build an ark—a huge boat—that would save both people and animals from a worldwide flood. The Lord planned to wash away the wickedness of humanity, and Noah was the only righteous man of his time. He and his family repopulated humanity, while the animals from the ark spread out to continue their lines.

40. **Paul**: God's chosen apostle to the Gentiles. Originally called Saul, he zealously persecuted Christians until he became one after Jesus confronted him on the way to Damascus. Scripture begins calling him Paul when he and Barnabas set out on the first of his three missionary journeys. Paul communicated with many people through his epistles, or letters, that became books of the Bible. He wrote to the Romans,

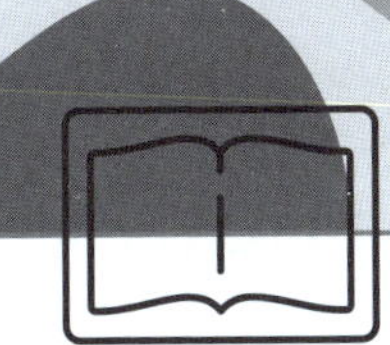

# Jesus' Original 12 Disciples

- Simon Peter
- Andrew, Peter's brother
- James, son of Zebedee
- John, brother of James and Jesus' closest friend
- Philip
- Bartholomew
- Thomas
- Matthew, also known as Levi
- James, son of Alphaeus
- Thaddaeus, also known as Lebbaeus and Judas, son of James
- Simon the Zealot
- Judas Iscariot, the betrayer of Jesus

Corinthians, Ephesians, Galatians, Philippians, Colossians, and Thessalonians, as well as to the individuals Titus, Timothy, and Philemon.

41. **Peter**: Also called Simon Peter and Simon Bar-Jonah, he was called from his profession of fishing to become a fisher of men. Along with his brother Andrew, Peter was among Jesus' most intimate disciples. After Jesus' ascension to heaven, Peter, filled with the Holy Spirit, spoke out boldly on the holiday called Pentecost, and three thousand people were saved. God gave Peter a vision about the acceptance of Gentile believers in the church. He wrote the New Testament books of 1 and 2 Peter.

42. **Ruth**: A pagan woman from Moab. Ruth married into a Jewish family that was living in Moab due to a famine around Jerusalem. When Ruth's husband, brother-in-law, and father-in-law all died, she refused to leave to her mother-in-law, Naomi. Having heard that the famine was over, they went to Bethlehem, where Ruth gleaned barley for food. The wealthy field owner took an interest in Ruth and married her. They started a family line that included both King David and Jesus Christ.

43. **Samson**: The twelfth judge of Israel. He was under a Nazarite vow from birth, meaning he

could not consume anything from a grapevine or cut his hair. God gave Samson amazing strength to defend his people from the enemy Philistines. But he was weak in character. Samson's lust for Delilah led to the cutting of his hair, the loss of his strength, and his imprisonment by the Philistines. Humbled, he made one final request of God and killed thousands of enemies—along with himself—by collapsing their temple.

44. **Samuel**: Prophet and judge of Israel. After young Samuel was weaned, his mother brought him to the tabernacle to live with Eli the priest and serve the Lord. God spoke to the boy in the night, and in his first prophecy, Samuel spoke out against Eli's wicked sons. Samuel led the Israelites spiritually, anointed the nation's first two kings, and judged Israel his whole life.

45. **Sarah**: The name God gave to Sarai, wife of Abram, after promising the old, barren couple that she would bear a child. When she was ninety, God repeated the promise to give Abraham a son by her. When Sarah heard this, she laughed—but a year later she gave birth to Isaac.

46. **Saul**: The first king of Israel. Anointed by the prophet Samuel, Saul started well with strong leadership and military victories. But when he made a burnt offering to God—a job reserved to the priests—Samuel told Saul that he would

lose his kingdom. When God ordered Saul to utterly destroy the Amalekites, Saul did not kill their king or their cattle. God rejected him as Israel's leader, and Samuel anointed young David to be king.

47. **Silas**: A church leader chosen by the Jerusalem Council to accompany Paul and Barnabas to preach to Gentiles. When Barnabas and Paul separated, the latter took Silas on a new missionary journey. They were imprisoned in Philippi after Paul freed a slave girl of an evil spirit, and they led the jailer and his family to Christ.

48. **Solomon**: Son of King David and his wife Bathsheba. Despite the efforts of his half brother Adonijah to take the throne, Solomon became king over Israel with the support of his father. When God visited Solomon in a vision, offering him anything he wanted, the young king requested an understanding heart to rule the people. God gave Solomon wisdom and understanding, along with wealth and honor he had not requested. Solomon built the Lord's temple in Jerusalem, then dedicated the facility with a memorable prayer.

49. **Stephen**: A Jewish man of the early church, said to be full of faith and the Holy Spirit.

Stephen was ordained as a deacon to care for the physical needs of church members. He spoke boldly to fellow Jews who accused him of blasphemy, and was stoned by an angry mob that included Saul of Tarsus, who later became the apostle Paul.

50. **Timothy**: Coworker and "son in the faith" of the apostle Paul. Timothy's name is joined with Paul's in the introductory greetings of 2 Corinthians, Philippians, Colossians, and Philemon. Paul also wrote two epistles of guidance to this young pastor.

# Fifty of the Most Important Places in the Bible

1. **Ai**: A city in the Promised Land that Joshua's spies reported had few inhabitants. Joshua sent three thousand men to conquer the city, but his soldiers fled before Ai's warriors. God told Joshua the failure was due to Israel's sin. Once Joshua identified and executed Achan, who had disobeyed a

command regarding Jericho, God commanded the Israelites to attack Ai again. This time, He would give it into their hands (see Joshua 7–8).

2. **Antioch**: Capital of Syria. The church in Jerusalem sent Barnabas to Antioch after word arrived that Gentiles were responding to the gospel. Barnabas first went to Tarsus, to take along the newly converted Saul. He and Barnabas received their missionary calling in Antioch, where believers were first called "Christians" (see Acts 11:19–26).

3. **Armageddon**: A symbolic name for the place the apostle John foretold will host the last great battle on earth, fought between Jesus and the antichrist (see Revelation 16:12–16).

4. **Asia**: A Roman province in the western part of the continent of Asia. Its capital was Ephesus. For a time, the Holy Spirit prohibited Paul from preaching in Asia (Acts 16:6–8), but he visited Ephesus on his second missionary journey and remained there two years. When Demetrius the silversmith started a riot over Paul's preaching in Ephesus, the apostle moved on to Macedonia (Acts 19). Peter wrote his first epistle in part to believers in Asia, and John addressed his Revelation to "the seven churches that are in Asia" (Revelation 1:4).

5. **Assyria**: An empire that ultimately incorporated a wide arc of land from Egypt, north through Syria and the Promised Land to eastern Asia Minor, and west to Babylonia

and the Persian Gulf. During the reign of Judah's King Manasseh, Assyria attacked, carrying him and many of his people to Babylon (2 Chronicles 33:11). When Manasseh humbled himself before God, he was returned to his position in Jerusalem. God promised that Assyria would be punished and a remnant of Judah would return to the Lord (Isaiah 10:12, 21).

6. **Athens**: An influential Greek city on the peninsula of Attica, Athens was famed for its culture and philosophy. The apostle Paul traveled there from Berea after Jews of Thessalonica had stirred up trouble for him. Distressed by Athens' widespread idolatry, Paul preached Christ in the synagogue. At the invitation of Athenian philosophers, he then spoke at Mars' Hill, the Areopagus, where some prominent people became believers (see Acts 17:15–34).

7. **Babylon**: An ancient Mesopotamian city on the Euphrates River, and later capital of the Babylonian Empire. Under King Nebuchadnezzar, Babylon ransacked Jerusalem and took many of its people captive around 586 BC. In the New Testament, Peter refers to a church at Babylon, and the book of Revelation uses the name as well. Babylon takes on a symbolic meaning as a fallen, sinful city.

8. **Bethany**: A village about two miles from Jerusalem. Bethany is best known as the

home of Jesus' friends Lazarus, Martha, and Mary. When Lazarus became ill, Jesus did not return to the village until after the man had died. Martha and Mary mourned the fact that Jesus had not been there to prevent their brother's death. But Jesus brought Lazarus back to life, causing the jealous chief priests to plot to kill Him (John 11). Mary of Bethany anointed Jesus with oil prior to His crucifixion (John 12:1–3).

9. **Bethlehem**: Also called "Bethlehem of Judea," to distinguish it from another Bethlehem northwest of Nazareth, this town south of Jerusalem was the birthplace of Jesus. The birth had been foretold by the prophet Micah, who called the town Bethlehem Ephrathah (Micah 5:2). Wise men visited young Jesus here, offering Him gifts of gold, frankincense, and myrrh. God then warned Joseph to take his family into Egypt to avoid the jealous King Herod's anger (Matthew 2:1–14).

10. **Caesarea Philippi**: A town northeast of Galilee, distinguished from the Caesarea built by Herod the Great on the Mediterranean coast. Here Jesus asked His disciples, "Who do men say that I am?" Then Jesus asked His followers who they said He was. Peter answered, "You are the Christ" (Mark 8:27–29).

11. **Cana**: A Galilean village where Jesus and His disciples attended a wedding. The Lord performed His first miracle here, turning water

into wine (John 2:1–11). Jesus' disciple Nathanael came from Cana.

12. **Canaan**: Land east of the Mediterranean Sea as far as the Jordan River, and from the Taurus Mountains in the north, going south beyond Gaza. Canaan included the areas later called Phoenicia, Palestine, and Syria. Its inhabitants were the descendants of Noah's grandson Canaan, including the Hittites, Jebusites, Amorites, Girgashites, Hivites, Arkites, Sinites, Arvadites, Zemarites, and Hamathites (Genesis 10:15–18). God brought Abram and his family from Ur of the Chaldees to Canaan. Promising they would become a great nation there, the Lord told Abram that his descendants would own the land.

13. **Capernaum**: Jesus chose this village on the Sea of Galilee's north shore as His ministry headquarters. He left Nazareth for Capernaum when Herod imprisoned John the Baptist, fulfilling Isaiah's prophecy that Zebulun (which was the tribe of Nazareth) and Naphtali (which was the tribe of Capernaum) would see a great light. Jesus taught in Capernaum's synagogue, and from here called several disciples—fishermen Peter, Andrew, James, and John, as well as the tax collector Matthew. Jesus performed many miracles here as well.

14. **Colosse**: A city in the Roman province of Phrygia, in Asia Minor. The apostle Paul wrote the book of Colossians to the Christians in Colosse (Colossians 1:2).

15. **Corinth**: A Greek city, trading center and capital of the Roman province of Achaia. The apostle Paul visited Corinth during his second missionary journey, after ministering in Athens. In Corinth Paul met fellow tentmakers Aquila and Priscilla, who became friends and coworkers with him. Paul preached in the Corinthian synagogue until the Jews there strongly opposed him. He wrote 1 and 2 Corinthians to the troubled church in this city. A third letter, written between the two that appear in scripture, was apparently not preserved.

16. **Damascus**: An ancient Syrian city, northeast of Tyre, that King David conquered. Following David's victory, Damascus paid Israel tribute (2 Samuel 8:1–6). A thousand years later, near Damascus, the Christian persecutor Saul was confronted by Jesus. Temporarily blinded, he was led into the city, where a man named Ananias healed him with God's power. Converted, Saul—soon to be known as Paul—began preaching Christ in the synagogues of Damascus (Acts 9:3–20).

17. **Eden**: A garden God planted for Adam to live

in, just after creation. It was filled with pleasant trees and plants for food, and docile animals that God told Adam to name. Adam and Eve were to care for Eden and follow a single command: not to eat of "the tree of the knowledge of good and evil." When they listened to Satan and disobeyed God's command, God sent Adam and Eve out of the garden (Genesis 2–3).

18. **Edom**: The land of Esau, who was also called Edom, inhabited by his descendants. Edom lay south of Moab and southeast of the Dead Sea. The prophet Jeremiah described the inhabitants of this mountainous nation as living "in the clefts of the rock, who hold the height of the hill" (Jeremiah 49:16). Edom was ruled by kings well before Israel established a kingly line. Refused permission to cross Edom on their way to the Promised Land, Israel traveled just beyond the edges of that nation.

19. **Ephesus**: Capital of the Roman province of Asia, in the western part of Asia Minor. On his way to Jerusalem, Paul stopped in Ephesus and spoke to the Jews in its synagogue. Apollos also preached in the city, but only knowing the baptism of John the Baptist. Priscilla and Aquila stepped in to teach him the way of God more completely (Acts 18:19–26). From prison in Rome, Paul wrote an epistle to the Ephesian church focusing on the need for unity in the body of Christ.

20. **Galatia**: A Roman province in the center of

Asia Minor. For a time, the Holy Spirit forbade Paul and Silas from preaching here. Later, Paul strengthened the disciples in the provinces of Galatia and Phrygia. The apostle reminded the church of Galatia that he first preached to them because of an illness he was experiencing (Galatians 4:13). Paul wrote to the Galatians to establish the authority for his apostleship, to counter the influence of false teachers who had swayed some away from the gospel, and to encourage the people to believe in salvation by grace.

21. **Galilee**: An area in the north of Israel that may originally have been in the inheritance of the tribe of Naphtali. Israel did not overpower the people who inhabited the area, so it became racially mixed, earning the name "Galilee of the Gentiles." In Nazareth, a city of Galilee, Mary received news that she would bear the Messiah. Following Jesus' birth and the family's flight into Egypt, Joseph received an angel's message that he should return to Israel. He brought his family to Galilee to avoid the rule of Archelaeus, a son of Herod the Great (Matthew 2:13–23).

22. **Gethsemane**: A garden on the Mount of Olives, across the Kidron Valley from Jerusalem. Jesus brought His disciples to Gethsemane where He prayed, asking His

Father to remove the cup of crucifixion from Him. Despite His deep sorrow, Jesus accepted His Father's will, while His closest disciples—Peter, James, and John—fell asleep. An armed crowd arrived to arrest Jesus as Judas Iscariot betrayed Him with a kiss. The disciples fled as their Master was led away to face the Sanhedrin, the Jewish ruling council (Matthew 26:36–56).

23. **Golgotha**: The place near Jerusalem where Jesus was crucified. Golgotha is mentioned by all the Gospel writers except Luke, who calls it by the Latin name *Calvary*. According to the book of Hebrews, Golgotha was beyond the walls of Jerusalem: "Jesus also suffered outside the city gate" (13:12 NIV). John adds that there was a garden there, and an unused tomb in which Jesus was buried (John 19:41–42).

24. **Jericho**: An ancient city west of the Jordan River. When the Israelites entered Canaan, their promised land, they crossed the Jordan near Jericho. God gave Joshua an unusual battle plan to take the city: For six days Israel's soldiers were to walk once around Jericho; on the seventh day they were to go around the city seven times, with the priests blowing their trumpets and carrying the ark of the covenant. When the priests made a long trumpet blast, the people should shout. The walls would collapse, and Jericho would be theirs (Joshua 6).

25. **Jerusalem**: The primary city of Israel, which played a huge part in biblical history. After King David passed the throne to his son Solomon, the new king built God's temple in Jerusalem. Centuries later, Jesus was crucified and resurrected at this city. After His ascension, on the day of Pentecost, the Holy Spirit filled believers in Jerusalem. Here Stephen became the first martyr of the church after preaching the gospel with power. Jerusalem remained important, even as the church spread beyond Israel.

26. **Joppa**: A Mediterranean seaport in the territory of the tribe of Dan. The king of Tyre shipped cedar logs to King Solomon through Joppa for his building projects in Jerusalem. Following the Babylonian exile, when the Jews rebuilt their temple, they used the same route for supplies. Hoping to escape God's command to go to Nineveh, the prophet Jonah went to Joppa, seeking a ship bound for Tarshish (Jonah 1:3). At Simon the tanner's house in Joppa, the apostle Peter saw a vision he understood as God's message that he should accept Gentiles who believed in Jesus (Acts 10:8–48).

27. **Jordan River**: The river flowing from northern Israel's Lake Huleh, south to the Sea of Galilee, and on to the Dead Sea. The Jordan River defined the eastern edge of Canaan. On their way toward their promised land, the Israelites conquered lands east of the Jordan. Following

the conquest of the Promised Land itself, most of Israel's territory lay west of the Jordan. John the Baptist performed baptisms in the Jordan River, including the baptism of Jesus (Matthew 3:6, 13–17).

28. **Kadesh**: A wilderness area south of the Dead Sea where Moses sent scouts to investigate the land of Canaan. They reported that the territory was fertile enough to support the people, but it was inhabited by powerful tribes entrenched behind walled cities (Numbers 13). At this news the people cried out against the Lord and Moses for leading them to what they perceived to be a dead end. God punished them for their disobedience by forcing them to wander in the wilderness for forty years until all the doubters were dead (Numbers 14).

29. **Laodicea**: A city of the Roman province of Phrygia. Paul's epistle to the Colossians was written to be read in both Colosse and Laodicea. The apostle John delivered a message from Jesus to the church at Laodicea, stating that the believers there had grown lukewarm (Revelation 3:14–22).

30. **Lystra**: A city of Lycaonia to which Paul and Barnabas fled after the Jews of Iconium tried to stone them. In Lystra, Paul healed a lame man, and the people responded by declaring Paul and Barnabas gods. But when Jews of Antioch and Iconium followed the apostles to Lystra, Paul was stoned (Acts 14:6–20).

The apostle miraculously survived, and he and Barnabas later returned to Lystra to encourage the believers. Christians of Lystra and Iconium gave a good report about Timothy, so Paul took him on his missionary travels.

31. **Midian**: A land east of the Sinai peninsula, in the northwest portion of Arabia. Moses fled here as a young man after killing an Egyptian (Exodus 2:11–15). He married Zipporah, daughter of Midian's priest, Jethro. When Israel conquered the Promised Land, Midianites sought to lure Israel into idolatry and intermarriage (Numbers 25).

32. **Moab**: This nation, composed of the descendants of Lot and his eldest daughter (Genesis 19:37), lay east of the Dead Sea. At God's command, Israel skirted Moab and went through Amorite territory on their way to the Promised Land. Moab's king, Balak, feared the Israelites and asked the pagan prophet Balaam to curse them. When Balaam could not, he counseled Balak to lead Israel into idolatry (Numbers 31:16). Moab periodically took up arms against God's people.

33. **Mount Carmel**: A notable mountain in northern Israel where Elijah confronted Israel's King Ahab and the priests of Baal (1 Kings 18:19–42).

34. **Mount Olivet**: Also called the Mount of Olives, it is a mountain ridge east of Jerusalem. King David fled here from his son Absalom, grieving as he ascended the Olivet ridge (2 Samuel 15:30). From this place, Jesus ascended into heaven. Luke describes it as "a Sabbath day's journey" outside the city (Acts 1:1–12).

35. **Mount Sinai**: A mountain in the south-central part of the peninsula between Egypt and the Promised Land. God called Moses to Mount Sinai and told him to sanctify the people (Exodus 19). Then Moses went up, alone, to receive the Law. Since he was gone for many days, the people became impatient and pressured Aaron into creating a calf-shaped idol of gold (Exodus 32). Enraged by what he saw, Moses broke the stone tablets of the covenant. After the idol was destroyed, God called Moses back to Mount Sinai to receive a new copy of the commandments (Exodus 34:1–2).

36. **Nazareth**: In this village of Galilee, the virgin Mary heard the news that she would bear the Messiah. After the death of Herod the Great, Joseph brought Mary and Jesus out of Egypt and back to live in Nazareth, which was beyond the reach of Archelaus, Herod the Great's son. Here Jesus announced the beginning of His ministry, saying He would fulfill the prophecy of liberty for God's people. The unbelieving townsfolk wanted to kill Him (Luke 4:28–29).

37. **Nile River**: This specific name does not appear in the King James or Simplified KJV, which simply say "the river." But some modern translations say the Nile River was the stream where Pharaoh's daughter found baby Moses floating in a basket (Exodus 2:3–5). It was also the site of some of the ten plagues (Exodus 7:15, 20).

38. **Nineveh**: An ancient city that became the capital of the Assyrian Empire. Nineveh was located on the Tigris River's eastern bank. When Assyria attacked Jerusalem, God killed the foreign troops and the frightened King Sennacherib returned to Nineveh. Another time, God sent Jonah to preach repentance to this wicked city; surprisingly, Nineveh's king declared that everyone should repent, and they did. So God withheld the destruction He had threatened (Jonah 3).

39. **Philadelphia**: A city of Asia Minor, home to one of the seven churches of the book of Revelation. Jesus commended and encouraged this church, which had kept His word and avoided denying His name. God would protect the believers from the trials that lay ahead. But the Lord also warned them to hold on to what they already had so they would not lose their crown (Revelation 3:7–13).

40. **Philippi**: A chief city of northeastern Macedonia that Paul and his fellow laborers visited to preach the gospel. Here Lydia became a convert, and a slave girl with a

spirit of divination was healed. But the slave's owners dragged Paul and Silas before the magistrates, and the two men were imprisoned. Their jailer was converted before these prisoners were released by the magistrates (Acts 16). Paul wrote to the Christians of Philippi while he was in Rome.

41. **Rephidim**: A campsite of the Israelites as they traveled to the Promised Land. There was nothing to drink here, so God moved Israel to Horeb, where Moses produced miraculous water by striking the rock. At Rephidim, the Israelites were attacked by the Amalekites. Moses oversaw the battle from a hilltop, and as long as his arms were raised, Israel prevailed. When he grew tired, Aaron and Hur stood beside him and held his hands up until Joshua won the battle (Exodus 17:8–13). Moses built an altar here and called it Jehovah-nissi, "God is my banner."

42. **Rome**: The capital of the Roman Empire and center of the New Testament world. Though its political influence dominated New Testament believers, the city of Rome is not frequently mentioned in scripture. Emperor Claudius commanded Jews to leave Rome, so Aquila and his wife, Priscilla, moved to Corinth, where they met the apostle Paul. He ultimately went to Rome as a prisoner. From this city, Paul wrote the epistles of Ephesians, Philippians, Colossians, 2 Timothy, and Philemon.

43. **Samaria**: A major city of Israel (the Northern Kingdom) built by King Omri from the ground up as the new capital of the nation (1 Kings 16:24–29). Samaria was also a region, one of three territories into which the land of Israel was divided in New Testament times. Samaria was situated between Judea in the south and Galilee in the north. On one of His trips through this territory, Jesus offered "living water" to a Samaritan woman who came to draw water from a public well (John 4:10).

44. **Sardis**: A city northeast of Ephesus, in Asia Minor's district of Lydia. It is only mentioned in Revelation, in the letter to the seven churches. Though the church at Sardis had a reputation for being alive in Christ, Jesus said they were dead and needed to repent. Only a few believers there were not defiled (Revelation 3:1–6).

45. **Shechem**: A place in the land of Canaan where Jacob bought land and built an altar called El-elohe-Israel (Genesis 33:18–20). Following Israel's conquest of the Promised Land, Shechem became one of six cities of refuge established for those who had committed accidental murder. It was given to the Levites by the tribe of Ephraim. At Shechem, Joshua gave his last address to the people of Israel, reminding them of their history and the faithfulness of God (Joshua 24).

46. **Shiloh**: A town in the territory of Ephraim where the Israelites assembled after the battles to conquer the Promised Land. They set up the worship center called the tabernacle here. The tabernacle remained at Shiloh until the time of the prophet Samuel. When Hannah, mother of the prophet Samuel, asked the Lord for a child, she went to Shiloh to pray (1 Samuel 1:1–28).

47. **Sodom**: One of five Canaanite "cities of the plain" that may have been at the southern end of the Dead Sea. Abram's nephew, Lot, chose this land when offered whatever area he preferred. Though the men of Sodom "were exceedingly wicked and sinners before the LORD" (Genesis 13:13), Lot pitched his tent near the city. When Abram learned that God planned to destroy Sodom for its sin, he bargained with the Lord, who agreed that if ten righteous people could be found in Sodom, it would be spared (Genesis 18:16–33). Sadly, not even ten were found, and Lot was warned to leave the city. Angels took Lot's family out of Sodom, and God destroyed it—along with Gomorrah—by fire and brimstone (Genesis 19:1–29).

48. **Thessalonica**: A Macedonian city where Paul preached in the synagogue. Though some people of the city believed, others accused Christians of believing in a king other than Caesar. Christians of the city sent

Paul and Silas away to Berea (Acts 17:1–9). Thessalonica was the hometown of Aristarchus, who sailed with Paul on his way to Rome.

49. **Tyre**: A fortified Phoenician port and center of trade. Tyre had two harbors on the Mediterranean, and consisted of both an island and a city on the mainland. King David and his son Solomon had a strong trade relationship with Tyre (1 Kings 5:1–12; 1 Chronicles 22:4). In New Testament times, people of Tyre heard of Jesus' miracles and came to see Him (Mark 3:8). When Jesus traveled to the vicinity of Tyre, a local woman insisted that He help her daughter, who had an unclean spirit. Commending her great faith, Jesus healed the girl (Matthew 15:21–28).

50. **Zion**: Originally the name of a fortified mound on one of Jerusalem's southern hills, Zion (or Mount Zion) became the name for the temple mount, then the city of Jerusalem, and even sometimes the whole nation of Israel. It is often used in a poetic sense that glorifies God and Israel's role in bringing about His purposes. Solomon brought the ark of the covenant to Zion (1 Kings 8), where it was placed in the temple on the place that tradition claims is Mount Moriah—where Abraham almost sacrificed Isaac.

# How We Got the BIBLE

Take a look for a minute at your personal Bible. Have you ever wondered who was responsible for recording all the wonderful stories, promises, commands, and words of encouragement found throughout? Did God just drop His Word into someone's hands and say, "There's your Bible"? Or did people long ago just sit around thinking about God and the things He'd said and done, and then just start writing?

The real story of how we got the books of our Bible is actually a lot more complicated—and interesting—than that. It's also a lot more inspiring, for it demonstrates how God used ordinary, fallible people—just like us today—to give us His infallible written Word. More on those people later, but first let's consider how God used a group of people to do what no man could have done on his own.

More than forty men wrote the books we have in our Bible today. They came from a wide variety of backgrounds and vocations. In the Old Testament, for example, Moses was a shepherd, David a warrior and king, Ezra a priest, Isaiah (and many others) a prophet of God, and Amos a fig farmer. Similar variety can be found among the New Testament writers. Matthew was a tax collector; Peter and John were fishermen; Luke was a physician and historian; and the apostle Paul, once a devout Jewish religious leader, became a tentmaker.

Because all of us are imperfect people who live with other imperfect people, we know how hard it is to get three people—never mind more than forty—to agree on anything, let alone present consistent communication on a given subject. But the Bible never strays from its message, never contradicts itself, and always presents God's plan of redemption for humankind with perfect agreement.

But how did such a diverse group of writers—many of whom never met one another—pull that off? The answer lies in the word *inspiration*.

## When God Spoke, These People Listened—and Wrote!

As the apostle Paul declares, "All Scripture is given by inspiration of God" (2 Timothy 3:16).

We know what it means to be "inspired" to do, say, or write something. Most artists, poets, musicians, or novelists can point to their own work and tell you exactly what inspired them to make it. Emotions such as love, anger, hatred, or grief have inspired artistic types throughout the centuries.

But in the context of scripture, the word *inspiration* means more than just getting an idea or an inkling of what to say or write. It means more than seeing a need for a particular message and jotting it down. Inspiration means that God, through His Holy Spirit, spoke through a person, giving that person His very own words to record. In short, the people who wrote the books of the Bible were instruments that God miraculously used—pencils in His hand, as someone once put it—to give us His written Word, the Bible. That is precisely why some translations of the Bible render 2 Timothy 3:16 more literally, telling us that all scripture is "God-breathed." That means that God Himself breathed out the words you read in the pages of your Bible today.

The apostle Peter, who was with Jesus during His earthly ministry, expounds on this truth: "No prophecy of scripture is of any private interpretation. For the prophecy did not come in old time by the will of man, but holy men of God spoke as they were moved by the Holy Spirit" (2 Peter 1:20–21).

Although the Bible was written by dozens of fallible human beings, men from greatly diverse walks of life, it has one ultimate Author—God Himself. The Bible is both the history of God's interactions with His people and the rest of the world, and His instruction manual for living a life that pleases Him—also known as the life of faith. You can count on the Bible to be your ultimate source for everything you need to know, as relating to the life of faith and obedience to "the author and finisher of our faith" (Hebrews 12:2).

# How It All Started–the Old Testament

The Old Testament traces the story of humanity's start, the corruption of a once-perfect creation by sin, and how God set in motion the events that brought Jesus Christ to earth to rescue sinful people. The Old Testament is full of some of the most familiar characters and stories in the Bible, but more importantly, it demonstrates the power and care of a God who worked constantly (both up front and behind the scenes) to make sure His plan for redemption reached completion.

Following are thoughts on various authors and books of the Old Testament:

**Moses**: Though the book of Genesis doesn't name its author, long tradition holds that it was Moses, God's chosen man to lead the people of Israel out of Egyptian captivity. Moses is also credited with writing Exodus (see Exodus 17:14; 24:4–7; 34:27), Leviticus, Numbers, and Deuteronomy. Some also suggest that Moses recorded the book of Job, widely believed to be the oldest book in the Bible. Moses also authored one psalm, the ninetieth.

**Joshua**: The book of Joshua doesn't specify its author, but Jewish tradition and most modern Bible scholars hold that Joshua, Moses' successor as leader of Israel, recorded most of the book himself (see Joshua 24:26). The final section, describing Joshua's death and burial, were certainly added by someone else.

**Samuel**: Tradition holds that the prophet Samuel, the last of the judges who presided over the nation of Israel, authored the book of Judges. It is also possible, but not certain, that he wrote the book of Ruth and parts of 1 and 2 Samuel.

**Ezra and Nehemiah**: According to Jewish tradition, Ezra wrote parts of the book that bears his name, and also compiled and edited 1 and 2 Chronicles. Ezra had led a second wave of exiles back to Judah after the Babylonian captivity (around 605–530 BC), serving as priest for the people while Nehemiah acted as governor. Either man may have authored the book of Nehemiah, which is widely thought to be Nehemiah's autobiography.

**Mordecai**: Though the book of Esther doesn't name its author, the most popular and lasting tradition says that Mordecai, a major character in the story, did. Another possible author is Nehemiah.

**The book of Job**: As mentioned earlier, Moses may have written Job's story, the account of the suffering of a righteous man who had done nothing to deserve it. Other possible authors are King Solomon or Job himself.

**Psalm writers**: While David wrote many of the psalms, he didn't author all of them. Biblical scholars believe that at least twelve writers contributed to the

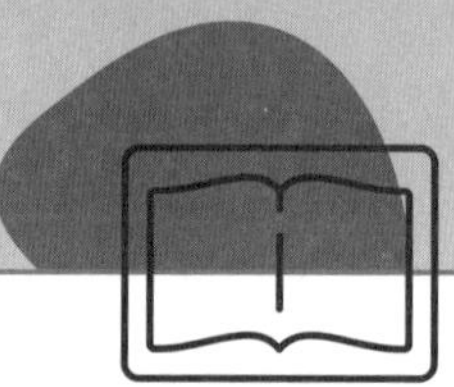

# The Minor Prophets

Don't let the term *minor* fool you. These twelve Old Testament men authored books containing shorter but still important prophecies—both in the short term, and much farther into the future.

**Hosea**: He compared the spiritual idolatry of God's people with the physical adultery of his own wife, Gomer.

**Joel**: Prophet of Judah (the Southern Kingdom) who used the devastation of a plague of locusts to call the people back to worshipping the one true God.

**Amos**: Prophet from a village in Judah who delivered the Lord's message to the affluent classes of Israel (the Northern Kingdom). Known as the great "prophet of righteousness," he foretold Israel's collapse and captivity by Assyria.

**Obadiah**: Prophet of Judah who condemned the Edomites for their mockery of Jerusalem.

**Jonah**: Prophet who was swallowed by a "great fish" while fleeing from God's call to preach to the pagan Assyrians. After God delivered Jonah from the fish, he did as directed, and many people turned to the Lord.

**Micah**: He was known for his prediction that Jesus the Messiah would be born in Bethlehem Ephratah, an ancient name for the city of Bethlehem.

**Nahum**: Prophet of Judah who announced God's forthcoming judgment against the pagan city of Nineveh.

**Habakkuk**: Prophet of Judah who was probably a contemporary of Jeremiah. He questioned the coming suffering and humiliation of God's people at the hands of the pagan Babylonians.

**Zephaniah**: Priest and friend of the prophet Jeremiah. Zephaniah often served as a messenger between Jeremiah and King Zedekiah of Judah. After Jerusalem fell, Zephaniah was killed by the Babylonians.

**Haggai**: Prophet after the Babylonian Exile. He encouraged the people to finish the task of rebuilding the temple because of its central role in their faith.

**Zechariah**: Prophet who delivered his messages to the people of Judah. Like Haggai, he encouraged the people to complete the task of rebuilding the temple in Jerusalem.

**Malachi**: Prophet who delivered God's message to the people of Judah. He warned against the shallow and meaningless worship practices of God's people after the Exile.

book—seven of whom we know by name. Of the 150 psalms, forty-eight are not ascribed to an individual writer. David wrote at least seventy-three, and it is likely that he penned some of those whose authors are unknown. Asaph, a music director during the reigns of kings David and Solomon, wrote a dozen psalms (50, 73–83), and another dozen are credited to the Sons of Korah, Levites who served in the temple (42–49, 84, 85, 87, 88). Solomon wrote two psalms that we know of (72, 127), but 1 Kings 4:29–32 indicates he wrote more than a thousand songs. Heman, Ethan, and Moses are also identified as writers of psalms.

**Solomon**: Israel's third monarch, the son of King David, is believed to have written the first twenty-nine chapters of Proverbs (Agur and Lemuel wrote the final two). Solomon may also have written Ecclesiastes and the Song of Solomon.

**Isaiah**: Isaiah, the son of Amoz, was a prophet who ministered to the people of Judah through the reigns of four different kings (around 740–681 BC). His book of prophecies is the Old Testament book most often quoted in the New Testament. Isaiah describes God's intolerance of sin, coming judgment for that sin, and hope of the Messiah who would provide atonement for human sin.

**Jeremiah**: Called the "weeping prophet" for the mournful tone of his messages describing the destruction of Jerusalem. Jeremiah penned a book of prophecies that bears his name, along with the companion book of Lamentations. According to Jewish tradition and many biblical scholars, Jeremiah may also have recorded 1 and 2 Kings. His prophecies cover the dark period in Judah's history from the reign of King Josiah (around 627 BC) to several years after the Babylonian invasion (586 BC), which Jeremiah foretold.

**Ezekiel**: The prophet and priest Ezekiel ministered to Judah just before and during the Babylonian captivity. His prophetic book is seen as a companion piece to that of Jeremiah, but Ezekiel focuses more on God's message of restoration for His people once they repent of their sin.

**Daniel**: Daniel recorded his life experiences and prophecies, which cover a time during and shortly after the Babylonian captivity. His prophecies foretold the coming of several key historic figures, such as Alexander the Great and, most importantly, Jesus Christ. They also foretell the coming of the Antichrist and the second coming of Jesus at the end of days.

## A New Era of Scripture Preservation

In 586 BC, Babylonians under the command of King Nebuchadnezzar sacked Jerusalem, looted and destroyed the temple, and took many of the city's people away from their home to Babylon. They would stay there for the next seventy years in what is called the Babylonian captivity.

During this captivity, certain Levites—men set apart for service in the tabernacle and, later, the temple—began copying the Jewish scriptures and distributing them to the other Israelites living in Babylon. These Levites came to be known as scribes. They gained distinction for their unsurpassed knowledge of the scriptures, as well as their accuracy in copying them.

The scribes followed a painstaking process, which had developed since the beginning of the monarchy in Israel. To faithfully reproduce copies of the books of the Law, they did their work by hand while following a meticulous set of regulations. These rules ensured that the job was done with complete accuracy.

## *Following a Process*

The Jewish scribes knew they weren't handling just any set of writings. These were the words of God Himself, and they approached their work with the diligence and passion due such an important calling. The scribes held fast to the rules for the transcribing, as recorded in the Talmud, the ancient record pertaining to Jewish law, ethics, customs, and history. Here is a quick overview of those rules:

- The scribe was required to prepare a parchment and dedicate it to the Lord before he began his work.
- Each column on the parchment could include no fewer than forty-eight lines and no more than sixty. Letters and words alike had to be spaced at a certain distance, and no word could touch another. This reduced confusion

in reading as well as errors in future copying.

- The ink used was always black and of a special mixture used only for copying scripture.
- Even if a scribe had memorized a passage of scripture, he was not allowed to write it down from memory. He was still required to check against an authentic copy of scripture. And, as he wrote, he had to pronounce every word out loud.
- Every time the scribe wrote the name of God, he was required to wipe his pen clean and wash his entire body. This was in reverence for God and for His Word.
- After the copying was completed, the scroll was to be examined and checked for accuracy within thirty days. If the scribe made even one error, the entire sheet on which the mistake was made was destroyed. If mistakes were found on three separate pages, the entire manuscript was condemned

The scribe counted every paragraph, word, and letter in the manuscript. Each had to correspond perfectly to the original. Once the process of copying was completed, the new manuscript could be stored only in sacred places, such as in a synagogue.

This exacting process of copying and recopying the Hebrew scriptures in ancient times led to reproductions of the Old Testament that held incredibly true to their original words and intent. Some estimates hold that copies of the Old Testament text used in translating the Bible into English were 99.9 percent true to the original—with the only deviations in being updated spelling and punctuation.

## Some "New Covenant" Writing

The Bible as a whole is the story of God's plan for the redemption of humankind. The Old Testament is the story of His "laying the groundwork" for bringing salvation to the world. Then the New Testament tells the story of how God sent His Son, Jesus Christ, to bring the news and do the work of that salvation (John 3:16). Much of the New Testament also explains what that gift means to individual believers.

To learn about Jesus and the beginning of the Christian church following His death and resurrection, look to the first five books of the New Testament—the four Gospels and the book of Acts. Here is some background on each author:

**Matthew**: Matthew was part of the most hated class of people in first-century Israel—tax collectors for the Roman government, whom the Jewish people saw as the worst of sinners. But when he heard Jesus' call to follow Him, Matthew immediately obeyed (see Matthew 9:9; Luke 5:27–28). He later wrote a

Gospel specifically targeting the first wave of Jewish Christians.

**Mark**: Most scholars believe the author of the second Gospel was a young man named John Mark, mentioned in the book of Acts as a traveling companion of the missionaries Paul and Barnabas (Acts 12:25). Many also think the unnamed, naked young man who fled the scene of Jesus' arrest in the Garden of Gethsemane was also John Mark (Mark 14:51–52).

**Luke**: Luke, a historian, physician, and missionary, wrote the third Gospel, as well as the book of Acts. Luke is unique among biblical writers in that he is the only Gentile (non-Jew) involved. It seems that Luke accompanied Paul in his later missionary journeys, because the pronouns change to say "we" (see Acts 16:11). Luke's skill as a historian and writer shows through his detailed accounts.

**John**: The writer of the fourth Gospel refers to himself as the disciple "whom Jesus loved" (John 13:23). John was a fisherman who became a disciple of Jesus and went on to write the Gospel of John, three epistles bearing his name (1, 2, and 3 John) and the book of Revelation.

# The Epistles: Words to Live By!

The next twenty-one books of the New Testament provide practical wisdom—commandments, guidelines, and promises—for living the Christian life. These letters, also known as "epistles," were written to various individuals, churches, and groups of believers to encourage, challenge, and instruct them in the faith life. There are five known writers of the New Testament epistles, including the apostle John.

Here are additional details on the writers and books that close out the New Testament:

**Paul**: From a human perspective, Paul is an unlikely "apostle of the Gentiles" (Romans 11:13) or author of the most New Testament books. Called Saul before his conversion, he had been a devout Jewish religious leader who was passionate about persecuting the new church (1 Timothy 1:13). But after a spectacular conversion experience on the road to Damascus, where he was headed to cause more trouble for Christians, Paul spent the remainder of his life faithfully following God's call to preach the gospel. He planted churches in cities around the region, and wrote letters to several churches that would become important books of the New Testament. He is known with certainty to have written Romans, 1 and 2 Corinthians, Galatians, Ephesians,

Philippians, Colossians, 1 and 2 Thessalonians, 1 and 2 Timothy, Titus, and Philemon. Some believe he also wrote the epistle to the Hebrews, but that isn't known for sure.

**Hebrews**: The authorship of Hebrews—the theme of which is the life, death, and resurrection of Jesus Christ, and how those events are related to Old Testament prophecies regarding the Messiah—remains a mystery. Some have speculated that Hebrews was another of Paul's epistles, though it differs notably from Paul's other letters. One obvious difference is that Paul identifies himself as the author in all thirteen of his epistles, but there is no name in Hebrews. Silas, Barnabas, Apollos, Luke, and Philip have also been suggested as the writer of Hebrews; and some even speculate that Priscilla, wife of the man named Aquila, wrote the book. If that were true, Priscilla would be the only female Bible author.

**James**: The New Testament mentions several men named James, but most scholars agree that the author of the epistle of James is "the Lord's brother" (Galatians 1:19; see also Mark 6:3), a son of Mary and Joseph.

**Peter**: Of the twelve men Jesus called to be His original disciples (see Matthew 4:18–20; Mark 1:16–18; Luke 5:1–11), none played a larger role in establishing the early church than Peter. This impetuous fisherman from the town of Bethsaida on the Sea of Galilee received and followed Jesus' call to be an apostle to the Jews. Peter preached with power following Jesus' return to heaven (Acts 2:14–39), and he wrote two epistles that bear his name.

**Jude**: The author of the second-to-last book of the Bible is not certain, but Jude (perhaps a shortened form of Judas) identifies himself as the brother of James (Jude 1). If he means the half brother of Jesus (see Mark 6:3), then Jude is humbly acknowledging his relationship to the Lord as well.

## Why These Books by These People?

All the writings that make up what we know as the Old Testament were completed by around 400 BC. All the books that comprise the New Testament were finished by the end of the first century AD. But the books included in our Bible weren't the only ones written concerning the history of the Jewish people, the life of Jesus, or the walk of faith in Christ.

That creates some questions for the average Bible reader. For example, how do we know that the Bible we have today says the same things the writers wrote thousands of years ago? And why were the books we now have in the Bible included, while others were left out?

Here's a look at how the Bible came together:

Writing to a young pastor named Timothy, the apostle Paul made an important statement: "All Scripture is God-breathed and is useful for teaching, rebuking, correcting and training in righteousness, so that the servant of God may be thoroughly equipped for every good work" (2 Timothy 3:16–17 NIV). This passage points out two key facts about the Word of God. First, God has clearly communicated every word you read in the Bible. Second, we can view the words of scripture as the promises and warnings, instructions and guidelines, that God knew we needed for a victorious life of faith.

But how can we know for sure that every word of every book in the Bible is indeed "God-breathed," and therefore "useful for teaching, rebuking, correcting and training in righteousness"?

The answer lies in the great care God put into making sure every word He inspired the biblical writers to record was kept safe over time. That work, of course, began with the Old Testament. The Hebrew scriptures—what we today call the Old Testament—were composed from about 1400 BC through around 400 BC, when the prophet Malachi finished his work. These books were written almost exclusively in Hebrew and were passed down from generation to generation of Jewish people, who from the time of their writing accepted them as the authentic, inspired Word of God.

Between 400 BC and the birth of Christ, several other books—what have come to be known as the Apocrypha—made their way into Jewish popular culture. But most Jews didn't accept these books as scripture, though many valued them as sources of history and some spiritual insight.

By the time of Jesus' birth, the "official" collection of Hebrew scriptures—called "the canon"—was pretty much decided. The Jews recognized that Moses, the prophets, and other writers were God's messengers, so their work was accepted as the inspired Word of God. By the mid-third century AD, the church was in almost complete agreement about the Hebrew canon of scripture.

## Many Were Written, but Few Were Chosen

By the end of the first century AD, every book of what would be known as the New Testament was completed. Depending on who wrote Hebrews, seven or eight people received the God-given words they recorded for the various churches and individuals to whom they ministered.

But there is evidence that these people also produced other writings which have long since been lost. For example, 1 Corinthians 5:9 tells us that the apostle Paul had written an earlier letter to the Corinthians. It's very possible that he, Peter, James, or other New Testament writers produced other writings not now included in our New Testament.

In addition to the "extra-biblical" writings of Bible writers, there were scores of documents from the first few centuries of Christianity that weren't included in the New Testament canon. Some were written too late

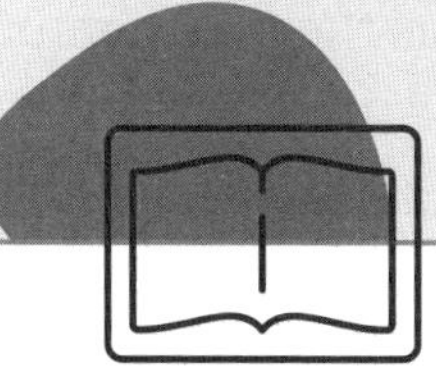

# What About the Apocrypha?

Many Roman Catholic Bibles contain several more Old Testament books than Protestant Bibles. These extra books make up what is referred to as the Apocrypha. They were mainly written in the years between Malachi, the last Old Testament book (approximately 400 BC), and the birth of Jesus Christ. The books in the Apocrypha include 1 and 2 Esdras, Tobit, Judith, Wisdom of Solomon, Ecclesiasticus, Baruch, the Letter of Jeremiah, Prayer of Manasseh, 1 and 2 Maccabees, and certain additions to Esther and Daniel—none of which were accepted into the Hebrew canon.

to be included, and others contained content that was questionable. Then there were writings by the earliest church leaders, such as the first-century bishop of Rome, Clement, who died around AD 99. He wrote a letter to the church at Corinth late in his life. Ignatius, a bishop of Antioch in Syria who lived to around AD 110, also sent letters to several churches and individuals.

Though the canon of the New Testament wasn't officially recognized—at least by any human institution—until the fourth century AD, the early church recognized the authenticity of certain letters and books far earlier than that. During the first few centuries of Christianity, the church had several criteria for recognizing a writing as being truly inspired by God. Some of these criteria applied to the writers themselves, and some applied to the writing—for example, did it tell the absolute truth about God, without contradiction or deceit? All the books the church recognized as inspired during those early years met those criteria.

The process of canonizing the New Testament books began during the times of the apostles. Some of them recognized one another's writings as inspired, and therefore scriptural. For example, the apostle Paul quoted the writings of Luke and referred to them as being scripture on a par with the Old Testament (see 1 Timothy 5:18; compare with Luke 10:7). Peter acknowledged that Paul's writings were truly inspired, even likening them to "the other scriptures" (2 Peter 3:16).

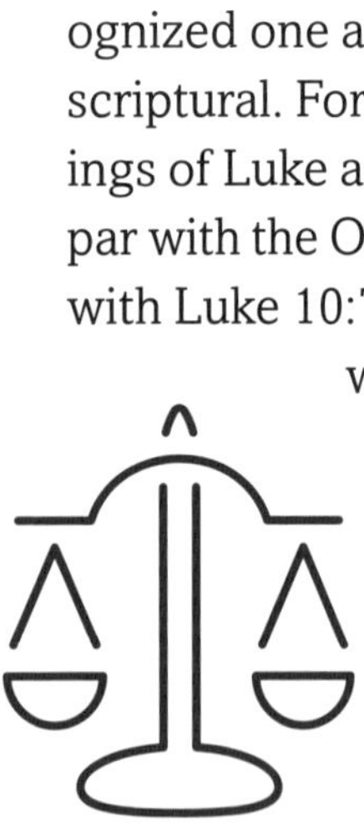

Early Christians immediately recognized the apostles as men God had appointed and gifted to communicate His Word to the world around them. That is why they obeyed the apostles' instructions to spread their writings to believers throughout the known world (see Colossians 4:16; 1 Thessalonians 5:27).

The process of acknowledging true New Testament scripture continued into the time of men known as the early church fathers—between the first and third centuries AD. Clement, in his writings, mentioned at least eight books that are included in the New Testament. Ignatius of Antioch acknowledged seven. Around AD 108 a man named Polycarp, a personal disciple of the apostle John, acknowledged fifteen New Testament books. The bishop of Lyon, Irenaeus, who lived around 130–200, mentioned twenty-two New Testament books, giving special attention to Paul's epistles.

In those days, efforts were occasionally made to compile an official canon of scripture. The first known list of New Testament books is called the "Muratorian Canon," which was discovered in the eighteenth century and is believed to date to the second century. It included all the New Testament books except Hebrews, James, and 3 John.

## Acknowledging What Is Already the Truth

As the faith began to expand and churches became more established, the rise in false teachers—as well as some Christians' acceptance of those teachers—moved faithful church leaders to realize that they needed to make a stand against those errors by formally acknowledging which writings were truly the inspired Word of God.

By the beginning of the fourth century, most of the books now in our New Testament had long been accepted as scripture. But a few still required further examination and approval before they could be declared part of the canon. Around AD 363, approximately thirty Christian leaders from Asia Minor met at the Council of Laodicea, where they decided that the Old Testament, including the Apocrypha, and the twenty-seven books in our New Testament could be read in the churches. The Council of Hippo in 393 and the Council of Carthage in 397 also affirmed the same twenty-seven books as the New Testament canon.

These councils didn't choose these books because they liked them best. The process of adopting the canon included putting each questionable book through thorough tests to make sure it deserved a place in the Bible. In the end, the councils acknowledged the collection of books we have in the New Testament today.

# The Canon of Scripture—Who Really Decided?

You've read about some events that led to the acceptance of the biblical canon. You've seen how what was once a list of countless documents was pared down until it became what we enjoy today: an error- and contradiction-free Bible that holds perfectly to God's message for humanity.

But how did such a large number of people—people with the same flaws and weaknesses we all have today—come to the agreement necessary to produce the perfect piece of work called "the Holy Bible"?

The answer lies in the guiding hand of God. Through the entire process of producing the Bible—from the actual writing of the scriptures to the church's recognition of those books God intended to comprise His written Word—you can see the Lord's hand. He was always working to ensure that His message would be exactly what He intended it to be.

No one man or single council simply chose the books for the canon of scripture. What was kept and what was discarded was a work of God Himself. Through the guidance of His Holy Spirit, God allowed people to understand which early Christian books were truly inspired, or "God-breathed." In other words, the choice of books we have in the Bible today was *God's* decision, not man's.

# Translation, Printing, and Publishing

Once the Bible canon was decided, it was necessary to get God's Word copied and into the hands of the people. Here are some important dates related to the story about Bible translating, printing, and distribution:

**AD 400**: Jerome completes the Latin Vulgate, a Greek manuscript containing the thirty-nine books of the Old Testament, the twenty-seven books of the New Testament, and the fourteen books of the Apocrypha.

**1227**: The Archbishop of Canterbury, Cardinal Stephen Langton, divides the Bible into chapters still used today.

**1384**: Death of John Wycliffe, who began translating the Bible into English. The work was completed after his death.

**1448**: The Hebrew Old Testament is divided into verses by a Jewish rabbi named Nathan.

**c. 1455**: German inventor Johannes Gutenberg develops the movable-type printing press, allowing for mass production of books. The Bible is the first book printed.

**1516**: Dutch theologian Desiderius Erasmus produces a Greek/Latin parallel New Testament.

**1522**: Martin Luther's German New Testament is published.

**1526**: William Tyndale's complete New Testament is the first printed in English.

**1534**: Martin Luther's complete German translation is published.

**1535**: Myles Coverdale publishes the first complete Bible in the English language.

**1539**: The "Great Bible," authorized by King Henry VIII, is the first English language Bible authorized for public use.

**1555**: French printer Robert Estienne divides the New Testament into standard, numbered verses. Along with Nathan's Old Testament verse numbers, the divisions have been accepted by nearly all following Bible versions.

**1560**: The Geneva Bible is the first English version to include both chapter and verse references.

**1611**: The King James Bible, including the Apocrypha, is printed; the Apocrypha is removed in 1885, leaving the sixty-six books we have today.

**1782**: Robert Aitken's Bible (the King James Version) is the first English language Bible printed in America.

**1885**: The "English Revised Version," the first major revision of the King James Version, is published.

**1900**: American publisher Thomas Nelson & Sons releases the American Standard Version

Old Testament; the following year, the company releases the entire Bible, the first major American revision of the King James.

**1952**: The Revised Standard Version is published.

**1965**: The Amplified Bible is published.

**1971**: The New American Standard Bible and The Living Bible are published.

**1978**: The complete New International Version is published.

**1982**: The complete New King James Version is published.

**1996**: The complete New Living Translation is published.

**2002**: The complete paraphrase known as The Message is published.

**2004**: The Holman Christian Standard Bible is published.

**2022**: Barbour Publishing introduces the Simplified KJV Bible.

# A Seven-Part BIBLE Outline

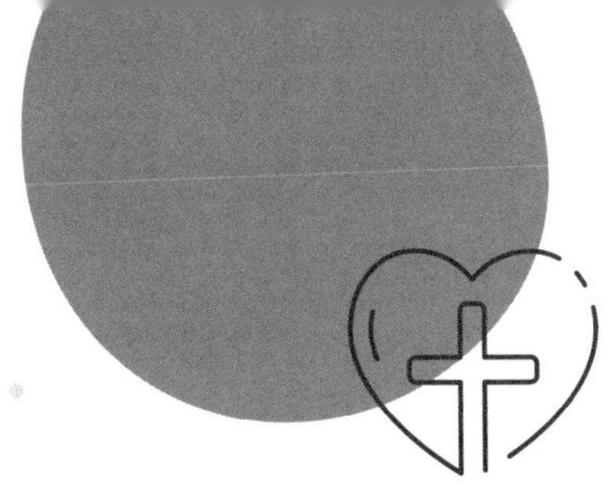

For a better understanding of the whole Bible, it's helpful to have a clear outline that breaks down the full story. That's what this chapter is all about.

Here is a seven-part outline giving you an overview of the big picture of God's Word:

1. **Creation**—where everything comes from
2. **Sin**—the problem that affects everyone
3. **God's People**—Israel as a blessing to all nations
4. **The Exile**—God's people in Babylon
5. **The Messiah**—Jesus arrives on earth
6. **Christianity**—How the church got its start
7. **The End Times**—Jesus' return and the renewal of all things

Ready to go? Let's dig deeper.

# Part 1: Creation—Where Everything Comes From

The book of Genesis, the very first book of the Bible, begins with the words, "In the beginning God created the heaven and the earth." On that first of six creation days, God made the earth (and the whole universe) out of nothing—nothing but His own words.

But after that first creation day, the world looked nothing like it later would.

On the first creation day (Genesis 1:1–5), God made the heavens and the earth, as well as light. He created the sky (our atmosphere) on day 2 (verses 6–8). On day 3 (verses 9–13), God fashioned dry land and made the very first living things—plants. On day 4 (verses 14–19), He created the sun, moon, and stars. On day 5 (verses 20–23), God introduced both water-dwelling creatures and birds to the earth. And on day 6 (verses 24–31), He created everything that lives on dry land, including human beings.

On the first five days of creation, God showed both His infinite power and His amazing creativity. But when He formed His most prized creation—human beings—He demonstrated His love. God spent the majority of creation week preparing the world, waiting until the sixth day to fashion a living being who could relate to Him in a deep, personal way—in much the same way a child relates to its loving parent.

God created every living thing on the earth, but we as human beings are the only ones He made in His own image. That doesn't imply that we're all-knowing and all-powerful like God is, but we reflect His nature, character, and personality in many important ways. For example, we can reason and communicate like He does, and we also have a creative side. Human beings were designed to rule over the earth and all the other living things God put here.

The Bible says that God "breathed into [man's] nose the breath of life" (Genesis 2:7 NLV). At that point, Adam gained not just physical life but a spirit and soul. He possessed the ability to do something none of the animals could: communicate with his Creator in a personal, loving way.

## God Designed Marriage

In creating human beings, God also created marriage. He looked at people, created as male and female, and said, "For this reason a man will leave his father and his mother, and will be joined to his wife. And they will become one flesh" (Genesis 2:24 NLV). Thousands of years later, Jesus quoted these very words when He was asked about marriage (see Matthew 19:4–6).

# Part 2: Sin–The Problem That Affects Everyone

Adam and Eve, the first people God created, had it made. God had placed them in a beautiful—really, a perfect—home. They had the run of the Garden of Eden, which their Creator visited every day. They could eat (almost) anything they wanted from the plant life that grew there. All they had to do was enjoy the garden and have a lot of kids. There was no sin or death—in fact, they didn't even know what sin or death were, because no one had ever sinned or died or suffered in any way. God intended for Adam and Eve to live like this forever.

God had given the first couple just one rule to follow: "Of every tree of the garden you may freely eat, but of the tree of the knowledge of good and evil, you shall not eat of it, for at the time when you eat of it, you shall surely die" (Genesis 2:16–17).

Tragically, Adam and Eve chose to disobey.

## *The Saddest Day in History*

The first humans had nothing to fear because they lived in perfect peace with God, as well as with the animals that also inhabited the garden. But one day as Eve was by herself in the garden, she was approached by a talking serpent—actually the devil in a snake's guise.

Though the woman knew God had forbidden people

from eating one tree's fruit, she listened as the snake told her, "No, you for sure will not die! For God knows that when you eat from it, your eyes will be opened and you will be like God, knowing good and bad" (Genesis 3:4–5 NLV).

Eve was convinced. She picked a piece of the fruit and took a bite, then handed some to Adam. He too knew better—but he took the fruit from Eve's hand and ate it. And everything changed for the first couple.

After Adam and Eve disobeyed God, they suffered terrible consequences. But they weren't the only ones—their children and their children's children, and every other human being down to this day, would be born into sin. This is known as "original sin"—and it's the worst thing ever to happen to humanity. Sin affects everything about us, and it separates us from God. That's why Adam and Eve hid from Him after they disobeyed (Genesis 3:10).

At the moment Adam ate the forbidden fruit, human life changed profoundly. Adam and Eve suddenly both felt guilt and shame for the first time. They were embarrassed at walking around the garden without clothing, so they gathered fig leaves and made coverings to hide their nakedness.

Worst of all, for the first time since God had made them, Adam and Eve were afraid of Him—so fearful that they hid themselves when they heard Him coming. God asked Adam, "Where are you?" (Genesis 3:9 NLV). It wasn't because God didn't know—He wanted Adam to admit to what he'd done. Adam answered, "I heard the sound of You in the garden. I was afraid because I was without clothes. So I hid myself" (verse 10 NLV).

It was a terrible day for Adam and Eve, and for every

human being who would live after them. Though God had said they would die if they ate from that "tree of the knowledge of good and evil," Adam and Eve didn't immediately pass away, at least not physically. But when they chose to sin, they died *spiritually*—in the sense that their relationship with God was ruined. They'd never again enjoy the close relationship they'd been intended to have with their Creator.

## *God's Plan to Fix the Sin Problem*

Though the whole world was now under a curse because of Adam and Eve's sin, God didn't leave humanity without hope. He had a plan to bring people back to Himself. That plan was to one day send a Messiah—a Savior—into the world to rescue us from sin. On the same day He banished Adam and Eve from the Garden of Eden, God made the first of dozens of Old Testament prophecies regarding His Messiah:

> *Then the Lord God said to the snake, "Because you have done this, you will be hated and will suffer more than all cattle, and more than every animal of the field. You will go on your stomach and you will eat dust all the days of your life. And I will make you and the woman hate each other, and your seed and her seed will hate each other. He will crush your head, and you will crush his heel."*
>
> GENESIS 3:14–15 NLV

While the name *Jesus* and the word *Savior* don't appear in this passage, the idea is certainly there. Genesis 3:14–15

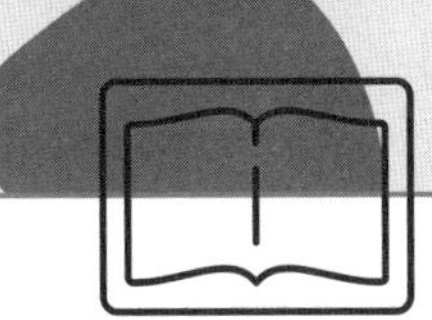

## Ever Wondered...?

Have you ever wondered why there are so many languages in the world? The Bible has the answer: Thousands of years ago, people tried to build a really tall tower (what came to be called "the Tower of Babel") that would reach heaven. God was not happy about that. To stop the work, He confused the people's language so they couldn't understand each other. Suddenly, the earth had different languages! You can read the whole story in Genesis 11:1–9.

indicates that God would send a Savior to be born from one of Eve's descendants—the Savior would be born from a mother just like every other person.

Adam and Eve had failed in the worst possible way. God punished them for their sin. But they were still the Lord's most prized creation. God would not simply let the devil have Adam and Eve—nor the people who would be born afterward.

In the meantime, though, sin and its consequences took a deadly hold on humanity. Genesis 4 reports how jealousy, anger, and even murder became a part of human life—starting with Adam and Eve's own children. In a fit of jealousy, Cain, the world's first child, killed his younger brother Abel, because God preferred the younger man's offering from the flocks over the older son's gifts of fruit and vegetables.

Going forward, humans only became more evil. Things got so bad that God decided to destroy the whole world—and every living thing on it—with a massive flood. The Lord instructed the world's only good man, Noah, to build a huge boat you know as "the ark." Noah and his family and two of every kind of animal would be saved from the flood, then repopulate the world after the water receded.

# Part 3: God's People—Israel as a Blessing to All Nations

The nation of Israel plays a huge role in the Bible because it played a huge role in God's plan to bring salvation to the world. Scripture shows that Israel was very special to God. Starting in Genesis 12, the Bible shows how God began to establish the nation of Israel, which would one day produce the Messiah.

Israel's earliest days are defined by what has been called "patriarchal history." The word *patriarch* means "father," and those of Genesis are Abraham (Genesis 11:26–25:8), Isaac (21:1–35:28), and Jacob, whom God renamed "Israel" (25:21–50:14). When we call these men patriarchs, we're really calling them the fathers of the nation of Israel. . .like George Washington was "the father of his country."

The man God chose to be father of Israel, and the spiritual father of Jews and Christians alike, was Abraham, who was originally called Abram. He is one of the most important people in scripture.

God called Abram, commanding him to leave his home country of Ur and travel "to a land that I will show you" (Genesis 12:1). That land was Canaan, about six hundred miles from where Abram was living. God promised to make this man into a great nation, even though he had no children of his own at the time. Abram did as God told him, gathering his wife and extended family and hitting the road.

Later, God promised Abram a son who would become the father of many descendants. That son was Isaac, who had twins named Esau and Jacob. Jacob, the younger twin, was later renamed Israel. He became the father of twelve sons, who would be patriarchs of large people groups known as "the twelve tribes of Israel."

Jacob's eleventh son was Joseph, who ended up in Egypt after his jealous older brothers sold him into slavery. In spite of his hardships, Joseph continued to honor God—who blessed the young man with great power, authority, and acclaim. By God's wisdom, Joseph explained a strange dream of Pharaoh, the Egyptian king, which indicated a famine was coming. Thanks to Joseph's wise counsel, Egypt stored up plenty of grain for the time of shortage.

Back in Canaan, the "Promised Land" that would become known as Israel, the famine was causing fear. When Jacob heard there was food in Egypt, he sent his older sons to purchase what they could. They appeared before Joseph, not realizing he was the brother they had treated so badly years before.

Ultimately, Joseph forgave his brothers and arranged for his extended family to join him in Egypt. Jacob, who had thought for years that his beloved son was dead, was shocked and overjoyed to see him again. Seventy members of the family settled Egypt, enjoying plenty of food and Joseph's protection.

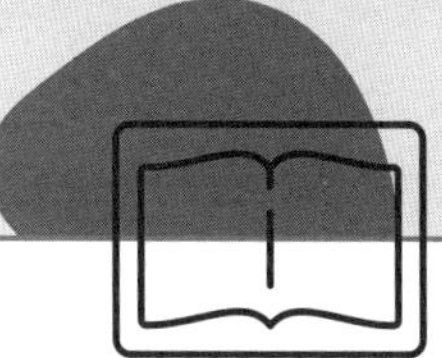

# The Ten Plagues of Egypt

1. Water turned to blood (Exodus 7:17–18)
2. Frogs (Exodus 8:1–4)
3. Lice (Exodus 8:16–17)
4. Flies (Exodus 8:20–22)
5. The death of livestock (Exodus 9:1–4)
6. Sores on people and animals (Exodus 9:8–9)
7. Hail (Exodus 9:22–23)
8. Locusts (Exodus 10:4–5)
9. Darkness (Exodus 10:21–22)
10. The death of all firstborn (Exodus 11:4–7)

## *Life in Egypt*

The Israelites lived in a part of Egypt called Goshen for about 430 years. During that time, they built homes, married, and had children—*lots* of children. For many years, the Israelites (also known as Hebrews) had it good in Egypt. But as their numbers grew, a new Pharaoh started to worry. Fearing that the Israelites would become too powerful to control—or might side even with Egypt's enemies in a war—Pharaoh enslaved God's people. He made them build cities and roads for him, working them hard in hopes of slowing their population growth.

God saw His people's suffering. The Israelites were still His chosen nation, and when the time was right, He called a man named Moses to lead the people out of their bondage. Moses was an Israelite, born during their slavery in Egypt. He miraculously escaped Pharaoh's command to drown male Hebrew babies in the Nile. Even more miraculously, he was adopted by Pharaoh's daughter! Growing up in the Egyptian palace, Moses still recognized his Israelite heritage. One day, he killed an Egyptian taskmaster who was abusing a Hebrew slave. Moses then fled for his life to a place called Midian.

After forty years there, Moses met God in a burning bush. The Lord told Moses to travel back to Egypt to demand that Pharaoh let the Israelites go free. Moses and his brother, Aaron, confronted Pharaoh, who stubbornly resisted. But after God sent ten devastating plagues on Egypt, Pharaoh let the Israelites go.

Moses led the Israelites out of Egypt, right through the Red Sea, which miraculously parted for them. Fear and sin turned the people's relatively short journey to the Promised Land into a forty-year wilderness wandering.

During that time, Moses received the laws God wanted His people to follow (the Ten Commandments, as well as many others) and wrote the first five books of the Bible—Genesis, Exodus, Leviticus, Numbers, and Deuteronomy.

Shortly before Moses' death, God commanded him to assign Joshua the position of national leadership (Deuteronomy 31:14). Joshua proved to be a strong leader, courageously leading the Israelites into the Promised Land.

The book of Joshua tells how Israel entered and conquered the promised land of Canaan. Chapter 6 describes the strange battle plan (God's plan) for neutralizing the enemy city of Jericho. In time, with Joshua leading the charge, the Israelites subdued all of southern Canaan (chapters 9–10), then defeated a coalition of northern Canaanite kings (chapter 11).

Though the Israelites had traveled as a group since leaving Egypt, they were still a collection of twelve tribes. Joshua's final duty was to assign each tribe its own section of the Promised Land. That story is told in Joshua 13–21. The great leader then died at the age of 110, and was buried in a place called Timnath-serah.

## *Special Deliverers*

The book of Judges describes leaders who bravely stepped up when the people of Israel—due to their own disobedience—were oppressed by foreign powers. Thirteen judges are named in the book of Judges, while two others followed in 1 Samuel. The time of the judges lasted around 350 years, starting sometime after 1400 BC.

In the judges' day, Israel had no human king. *God* was King, though the people often strayed from Him. So He raised up the judges to take responsibility for the nation. The book of Judges describes a dreary cycle: The people would follow God for a while, then fall away. God would allow other nations to dominate the Israelites until they cried out to Him. Then He would send a judge to deliver them from their enemies. This pattern repeated several times.

Deborah stands out as the only female judge of Israel. Gideon is famed for testing God's will with a fleece. But the best known of the judges is probably Samson, the deeply flawed strong man who battled the dreaded Philistines on behalf of his people.

## *Prophets and Kings*

The book of 1 Samuel, which follows shortly after the book of Judges, tells two major stories. The first is the account of the beloved prophet Samuel, Israel's last judge (chapters 1–12). The rest of the book describes the establishment of a monarchy—a government led by a king—in Israel. The people cried out for a king, wanting to be like other nations. God warned the people, his gave them what they wanted. Samuel anointed a man named Saul to be king, but his reign ended very badly for Israel. God then chose the young shepherd David to replace Saul.

David accomplished much for God and for the kingdom of Israel. He unified the twelve tribes into one great and powerful nation, making Jerusalem its capital city. David is considered Israel's greatest king—a good leader of the government, the military, and the nation's spiritual condition. He wrote nearly half of the psalms

# The Judges of Israel

- Othniel (Judges 3:7–11)
- Ehud (Judges 3:12–30)
- Shamgar (Judges 3:31)
- Deborah (Judges 4–5)
- Gideon (Judges 6–8)
- Abimelech (Judges 9)
- Tola (Judges 10:1–2)
- Jair (Judges 10:3–5)
- Jephthah (Judges 10:6–12:7)
- Ibzan (Judges 12:8–10)
- Elon (Judges 12:11–12)
- Abdon (Judges 12:13–15)
- Samson (Judges 13–16)
- Eli (1 Samuel 1–4:18)
- Samuel (1 Samuel 7:15)

in the Bible. Most importantly, David was known as a "man after God's own heart" who—despite his many flaws and failures—loved and served the Lord. He was an ancestor of the Messiah, Jesus Christ.

David, whose story is recorded in 2 Samuel and 1 Chronicles 11–29, served as Israel's king for forty years. After he died, his son Solomon took the throne. Very early in his reign, Solomon saw God in a dream. When the Lord asked him what he wanted, Solomon replied, "an understanding heart," which God was happy to give (see 1 Kings 3:6–15).

Solomon made the construction of a temple in Jerusalem his first priority. He dedicated himself and his nation's best resources to honor God with a spectacular building. Meanwhile, he became the richest and most powerful king in the world. These were blessings God gave Solomon in addition to wisdom.

Israel was flying high during Solomon's reign, but the good times didn't last. Solomon had been promised that his kingdom would last forever, as long as he followed God like his father David had done. God warned Solomon not to turn away—otherwise, terrible things would happen (1 Kings 9:6–9). Sadly, Solomon did eventually fail.

## *The Kingdom Divides—and Falls*

Solomon's many failures eventually led to Israel dividing into two rival nations—a northern kingdom still called Israel and a southern kingdom known as Judah. Israel was led by a series of kings, none of whom served the Lord. Judah did slightly better, but only a few of its kings followed God faithfully.

Israel fell into idolatry under its first king's leadership.

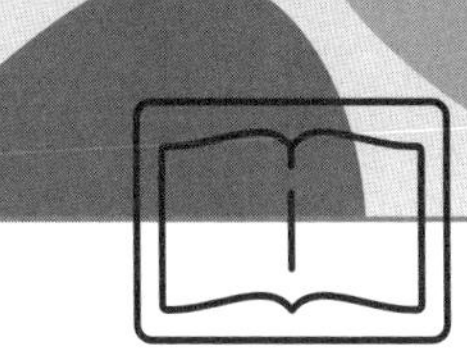

# Rulers of Judah (Southern Kingdom) in order

Rehoboam (c. 930–913 BC) / Abijah (c. 913–910 BC) / Asa (c. 910–872 BC) / Jehoshaphat (c. 872–853 BC) / Jehoram (c. 853–841 BC) / Ahaziah (c. 841 BC) / Athaliah (the only ruling queen, c. 841–835 BC) / Joash (c. 835–796 BC) / Amaziah (c. 796–792 BC) / Uzziah (also known as Azariah, c. 792–750 BC) / Jotham (c. 750–735 BC) / Ahaz (c. 735–715 BC) / Hezekiah (c. 715–687 BC) / Manasseh (c. 687–642 BC) / Amon (c. 642–640 BC) / Josiah (c. 640–609 BC) / Jehoahaz (c. 609 BC) / Jehoiakim (c. 609–598 BC) / Jehoiachin (c. 598–597 BC) / Zedekiah (c. 597–586 BC)

# Rulers of Israel (Northern Kingdom) in order

Jeroboam I (c. 930–909 BC) / Nadab (c. 909–908 BC) / Baasha (c. 908–886 BC) / Elah (c. 886–885 BC) / Zimri (c. 885 BC) / Tibni (c. 885–880 BC), rival rule with Omri (c. 885–874 BC) / Ahab (c. 874–853 BC) / Ahaziah (c. 853–852 BC) / Joram (c. 852–841 BC) / Jehu (c. 841–814 BC) / Jehoahaz (c. 814–798 BC) / Jehoash (c. 798–783 BC) / Jeroboam II (c. 783–753 BC) / Zechariah (c. 753–752 BC) / Shallum (c. 752 BC) / Menahem (c. 752–742 BC) / Pekahiah (c. 742–740 BC) / Pekah (c. 740–732 BC) / Hoshea (c. 732–722 BC)

Jeroboam feared that his people would travel to Jerusalem to worship God, and perhaps lose their loyalty to him. So he built two golden idols, in Bethel and Dan—essentially the farthest northern and southern points of his kingdom.

Rehoboam also failed as a leader in Judah. His father, Solomon, had built the magnificent temple to honor God. But during Rehoboam's reign, the people angered God by following many false gods. Rehoboam did nothing to bring his people back to the one true God.

## *Israel and Judah Warned of Judgment*

God repeatedly warned His people to turn from their idolatry and back to Him. The prophets Elijah and Elisha both preached repentance to the northern kingdom of Israel. The prophetic books of Hosea (13:16) and Micah (1:6) foretold in writing the destruction of Samaria, Israel's capital. Amos also foretold the destruction of the northern kingdom, and Isaiah prophesied that God would use the Assyrian Empire to punish Israel for its idolatry (Isaiah 10:5–19).

But the people of Israel refused to heed the prophets, and beginning around 733 BC, Assyrian forces invaded the northern regions and took many people captive. In 721 BC, Assyria attacked Samaria, Israel's capital, which fell three years later (2 Kings 18:9–12).

While the leaders of Israel were all wicked, Judah's kings had a slightly better record. Of Judah's twenty monarchs, about a third did well in serving the Lord. But even some of the good kings—such as Asa, Jehoshaphat, Joash, Amaziah, Uzziah, Jotham, Hezekiah, and Josiah—made serious mistakes at some point.

After the death of Josiah, Judah's last good king,

Judah was ruled by a series of ungodly men: Jehoahaz, Jehoiakim, Jehoiachin, and Zedekiah. None of these men loved or served God, and under their leadership the people of the southern kingdom fell further into disobedience.

God sent many prophets to warn Judah that judgment was coming. One of the "major prophets" (so named for the length of their books), Jeremiah, shared mostly bad news. God had given the people warning after warning, but they wouldn't listen. Now destruction was coming. Jeremiah, who faithfully carried God's message and suffered at the hands of his own people, would witness the utter destruction of Jerusalem.

# Part 4: The Exile—God's People in Babylon

Though God sent many prophets over many years to warn the people of Judah to turn from their idolatry and rebellion, they didn't listen. So God sent judgment on Judah several decades after Israel fell. Babylon exacted judgment on the Lord's people.

Babylonians came against Judah and Jerusalem in three different waves. In the first, around 607 BC, they captured many of Judah's bright young people (including a man named Daniel) and carted them back to Babylon. The second wave, 598–597 BC, included the capture of

King Jehoiachin, who was also taken away to Babylon. The third wave, around 586 BC, destroyed Jerusalem and its walls, burned the temple to the ground, and carried the temple's treasures back to Babylon (2 Kings 24:13).

Jeremiah had spoken God's warnings to Judah, and the prophet knew that the aftermath of the Babylonian attacks would be horrific. What he saw broke his heart. Jeremiah recorded his account of the destruction in what became the book of Lamentations.

Ezekiel was one of many Jewish people carried off to Babylon. He preached to his fellow captives of God's promise to one day restore their nation and bring them back to their homeland. Daniel too lived in Babylon during the captivity. Though he served among people who didn't know the Lord, Daniel remained faithful, recording prophecies and personal experiences while longing for Judah. Daniel wrote that God would bring His people back to Jerusalem after seventy years in exile.

God fulfilled that promise after the Persian king Cyrus the Great conquered Babylon in 539 BC. The book of Ezra shows God bringing the Jews back to their homeland after seven decades of captivity. Cyrus issued an order allowing the Jews to return to Judah. For his kindness and respect, he is respected by the Jewish people to this day.

After Cyrus' order, three waves of former captives traveled nine hundred miles from Babylon to Judah, where they quickly rebuilt Jerusalem's city walls. But they were slow to build a temple to replace the one the Babylonians had destroyed. The Jews laid a foundation and then stopped, troubled by enemy opposition. Through the prophets Haggai and Zechariah, God encouraged the people to finish the new temple, which they did around 516 BC.

About a century after the Babylonian Exile ended, Malachi wrote to the Jews in Jerusalem. They thought they were pleasing God, but their hearts were far from Him—so God demanded that they correct their attitude. Malachi's prophecy closed out the Old Testament; there would follow four hundred years of silence from God. This silence was broken when John the Baptist proclaimed the Messiah's arrival, and the New Testament era began.

# Part 5: The Messiah—Jesus Arrives on Earth

Though you won't find the name *Jesus* in the Old Testament, the Jewish Bible really is all about Him. Throughout the history of God's chosen people, the Lord spoke through many men to give the Jews promises of a coming Messiah.

The Old Testament includes predictions—all of which were fulfilled in Jesus—concerning the Messiah's virgin birth (Isaiah 7:14), where He would be born (Micah 5:2), that He would teach in parables (Psalm 78:1–2), that He would perform healings and other miracles (Isaiah 35:5–6), that He would suffer and die for His people (Isaiah 53), and that He would be raised from the dead (Psalm 118:17–18), among many others. Some experts count more than three hundred prophecies about Jesus in the Old Testament.

The New Testament begins with four books detailing

the life of Jesus—from His birth through His ministry on earth through His death and resurrection and return to heaven. These "Gospels"—Matthew, Mark, Luke, and John—each tell the same story but from a different perspective. Matthew, for example, takes a Jewish perspective, focusing on Jesus as the fulfillment of Old Testament prophecies of the Messiah. Mark emphasizes Jesus' power and work on earth, while Luke presents Him as the Savior for all people—Jews and Gentiles alike. John highlights Jesus as the Son of God, "the Word" who "was made flesh" (John 1:14).

Of the four Gospel accounts, only Matthew and Luke say anything about Jesus' arrival in this world or His childhood. Matthew wrote that Jesus' mother, Mary, "had been promised in marriage to Joseph. Before they were married, it was learned that she was to have a baby by the Holy Spirit" (1:18 NLV). Luke gives more detail about the birth of Jesus, reporting that the angel Gabriel visited Mary to announce that she would miraculously conceive the Son of God.

The Bible gives only a few quick glimpses of Jesus' childhood: His circumcision and His presentation at the Jerusalem temple (Luke 2:21–40), the wise men's visit (Matthew 2:1–12), and His journey to Egypt and back (Matthew 2:13–23), all in His first couple of years. Luke describes Jesus' visit to the temple on Passover at age twelve (Luke 2:41–52).

## *Jesus' Ministry on Earth*

Not long before Jesus started His ministry, John the Baptist appeared on the scene to prepare people for their Messiah. John

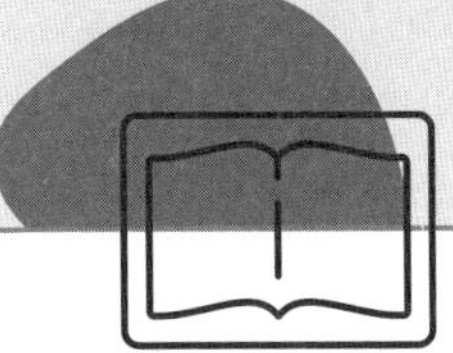

# Seven "I Am's" of Jesus

In the Gospel of John, Jesus makes seven powerful statements that reveal who He really is:

1. "I am the bread of life" (John 6:35)
2. "I am the light of the world" (John 8:12)
3. "I am the door of the sheep" (John 10:7)
4. "I am the good shepherd" (John 10:11)
5. "I am the resurrection and the life" (John 11:25)
6. "I am the way, the truth, and the life" (John 14:6)
7. "I am the true vine" (John 15:1)

peached that people should turn away from their sins to prepare their hearts for their long-awaited Savior.

John baptized Jesus in the Jordan River. Then the devil tempted Jesus in the wilderness. Soon afterward, Jesus called twelve men to follow Him so they could witness His amazing works, learn from His life-changing teaching, and be prepared for the work He would assign them to do after He returned to heaven to be with His Father. These men are "the twelve disciples": Peter, Andrew, James, John, Philip, Bartholomew (or Nathanael), Matthew, Thomas, James the son of Alphaeus, Simon the Zealot, Thaddaeus, and Judas Iscariot (Matthew 10:1–4; Luke 6:12–16).

Jesus taught and preached with great power and authority, performed stunning miracles, and demonstrated His power over sickness and death. After three years traveling the land of Israel on foot, He completed His ultimate mission when He was arrested, tried, and executed on a Roman cross. Jesus was crucified with criminals on either side of Him.

He was buried in a tomb owned by one of His followers. But Jesus didn't stay in the grave. Three days after His burial, His followers discovered that the tomb was empty. Jesus was alive! Over the next forty days, He would show Himself to His disciples and many other people who followed Him. Then, just before returning to heaven, Jesus gave His disciples the assignment they would carry out for Him—the "great commission" (see Matthew 28:18–20).

The disciples would do just as Jesus commanded them. Much of their work is described in the book of Acts.

# Part 6: Christianity—How the Church Got Its Start

The book of Acts—also called "The Acts of the Apostles"—is an account of the early church, beginning with Jesus' return to heaven. It tells of the first generation of Christians, especially the apostles. They were empowered by God's gift of the Holy Spirit (Acts 2) to take the message of salvation to Jerusalem, Judea, Samaria, and the surrounding world.

After Jesus was raised from the dead, He stayed on earth for forty days. During that time, He visited the apostles several times, proving to them that He really was alive and giving them final teachings about the kingdom of God. From the village of Bethany, on the Mount of Olives, Jesus told His followers to stay in Jerusalem until God sent the Holy Spirit (Acts 1:4–5), who would give them supernatural power (verse 8). After that, Jesus ascended up into the sky and on to heaven.

Jesus had promised His disciples that He would send them a "helper" after He left the earth. That helper was the Holy Spirit. God kept Jesus' promise on a Jewish holiday called Pentecost (Acts 2:1). As the believers were gathered in a house in Jerusalem, God sent the sound of violent wind and what appeared to be tongues of fire that came to rest on each one. These followers of Jesus began "to speak with other tongues"—languages they didn't know but that were heard and understood by the many visitors to the city (verses 9–10). The early Christians had all been filled with God's Holy Spirit.

The apostle Peter, empowered by the Spirit, courageously preached one of the Bible's greatest sermons (Acts 2:14–47). The Lord brought about three thousand people to faith in Jesus Christ that day (verse 41).

The new church—meaning the believers who lived in Jerusalem—began growing like wildfire. That led to a persecution of the apostles and other believers. The first Christian to lose his life for the faith was a man named Stephen, who was "full of God's grace and power" and who "performed great wonders and signs among the people" (Acts 6:8 NIV).

Stephen had spoken courageously to the Jewish high council in Jerusalem, condemning them for crucifying the Messiah. They were so furious that they stoned Stephen to death (Acts 7:54–60). As this first Christian martyr breathed his last, the Bible says a man named Saul looked on in approval.

Stephen's death touched off a huge wave of persecution against the church in Jerusalem. All the Christians except for the apostles fled the city, scattering throughout Judea and Samaria and preaching the gospel as they went.

## *Jesus Calls Saul to Serve Him*

A Jewish religious leader named Saul had violently opposed Christians in Jerusalem and beyond. One day, as he traveled to the city of Damascus to arrest believers and bring them back to Jerusalem to be jailed or killed, he met Jesus. An intense light from heaven surrounded Saul. He fell to the ground, blinded. Jesus spoke to Saul, giving him a new direction for life. Soon to be known as Paul, this man would "proclaim [Jesus'] name to the Gentiles and their kings and to the people of Israel" (Acts 9:15 NIV).

When Saul arrived in Damascus, Christians there worried. They all knew the terrible things Saul had done to believers in and around Jerusalem. But a man named Ananias stood up for Saul and convinced the believers to accept him. Later, another man named Barnabas would do the same thing in other places.

### "Christians"

Today, a follower of Jesus Christ is usually called a "Christian." The word appears first in the book of Acts, which says, "The followers were first called Christians in Antioch" (11:26 NLV). Antioch, about three hundred miles north of Jerusalem, was a hub of the early Christian church.

In Antioch of Syria, a sort of headquarters for the early church, a group of godly "prophets and teachers" (Acts 13:1) were worshipping God and praying when the Holy Spirit spoke: "Set apart for me Barnabas and Saul for the work to which I have called them" (13:2 NIV). The leaders laid their hands on the two men—a sign of support and approval—and then sent them out to faraway places to preach Jesus.

Starting about AD 47, Paul dedicated his life to traveling and preaching about Jesus. During three missionary journeys, Paul covered about ten thousand miles sharing the good news of salvation in Jesus to countless people. He founded at least fourteen churches (and maybe as many as twenty). He also wrote many letters that became books of the Bible, instructing, challenging, and encouraging Christians to this day—including Romans, 1–2 Corinthians, Galatians, Ephesians, Philippians, and Colossians. Paul also mentored several people who continued his ministry after he was gone.

Many people came to faith in Jesus when Paul preached. But many others hated Paul and his message. He was beaten, imprisoned, and threatened because he wouldn't stop talking about Jesus. Paul ended his third missionary journey in Jerusalem, where he was arrested for preaching Christ. He was taken to a city called Caesarea, where he spent two years in custody. While on trial before the Roman governor, Festus, Paul demanded his right to be tried by Caesar in Rome. He ultimately sailed for Rome, an adventurous trip that included a shipwreck and the miraculous survival of all 276 people aboard.

Acts ends with Paul living under house arrest in Rome. He was largely free to do as he pleased, so he boldly preached and taught his visitors about Jesus. Though his biblical story ends with Paul in his own rented home (Acts 28:30), certain church traditions say he was ultimately beheaded by Roman authorities.

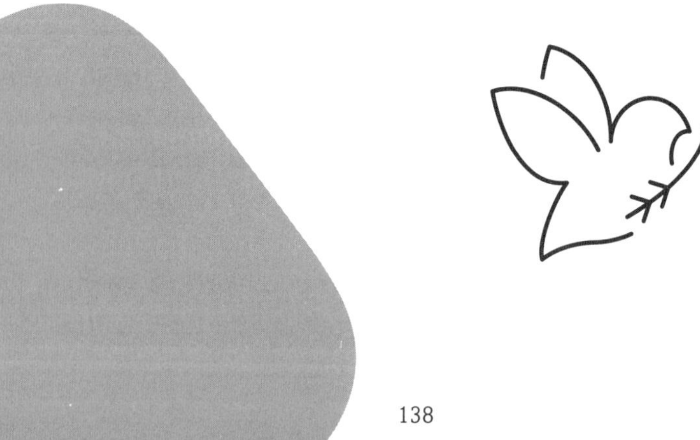

# Part 7: The End Times—Jesus' Return and the Renewal of All Things

The Bible repeatedly promises that Jesus will one day return to this lost, hurting, sinful world to mete out justice and make things right. Some of those promises came from the Lord's own mouth. For example, shortly before His crucifixion, Jesus told His disciples about His return (Matthew 24:30–31). Later, two angels promised that Jesus would return in the same way He had just ascended to heaven (Acts 1:10–11).

Though Jesus came to earth the first time as a suffering servant, He will return to earth as conquering King (Revelation 19:11–16). In John's book of Revelation, Jesus said, "I am coming soon!" (22:20 NLV). But shortly before He was arrested and crucified, Jesus told the disciples, "No one knows the day or the hour. No! Not even the angels in heaven know. The Son does not know. Only the Father knows" (Matthew 24:36 NLV).

We can't say exactly when Jesus will come back, and He never intended us to. But we can read the "signs of the times"—those events that indicate that His return is near. In His "Olivet Discourse" (Matthew 24–25; Mark 13; Luke 21), Jesus identified nearly two dozen signs that point to His nearing return. He encouraged believers to watch and remain faithful.

Revelation, the only book of prophecy in the New Testament, includes some scary end-times visions, including the rise of a person called "the Antichrist." The apostle Paul called him "that man of sin" and "the son of destruction" (2 Thessalonians 2:3). The Antichrist and his deeds are also described in Daniel 9:27 and 11:36–45.

Revelation 13 describes what is called "the mark of the beast" (or "the number of the beast") and a terrible time called the Great Tribulation. This is the awful time when God judges the entire world. The Bible says it will last seven years, and opinions differ on where Christians will be during this time. Some believe Jesus will take His followers to heaven before the tribulation in an event called the rapture. Others believe Christians will remain on earth for half of the tribulation. Still others believe Christians stay on earth the whole seven years

In Revelation 16, *Armageddon* refers to a future final battle between God and the forces of evil. In this place, God will destroy the armies of the Antichrist, as people from all nations will gather to fight against Jesus. With the Antichrist in command, the kings and leaders of earth will gather their forces for a massive assault on Jerusalem. But Jesus will stand on the Mount of Olives (Zechariah 14:4) with the armies of heaven at His command. He will defeat the forces of evil once and for all (Revelation 19:15–21).

The book of Revelation contains many disturbing—even frightening—images. There are terrible predictions of what will happen on earth in the end times. But Revelation ends with an uplifting, encouraging message: God wins! And so do those who follow Him.

For thousands of years, Satan has worked death and destruction on humankind. He's had quite a run, but the Bible says it will end. Here is Satan's future: "The devil who fooled them will be thrown into the lake of fire burning with sulphur. The wild animal and the false preacher are already there. They will all be punished day and night forever" (Revelation 20:10 NLV).

On the happier side of things, a new heaven and a new earth will take the place of the broken physical world. John wrote, "I saw the Holy City, the new Jerusalem. It was coming down out of heaven from God. It was made ready like a bride is made ready for her husband" (Revelation 21:2 NLV).

When this all happens, "God will take away all their tears. There will be no more death or sorrow or crying or pain. All the old things have passed away" (Revelation 21:4 NLV). From that moment on, the curse of sin will be gone forever (Revelation 22:3), and a perfect eternity begins.

What a great ending for the Bible's story!

# Jesus: The BIBLE'S Main Man

Speaking honestly and courageously to a group of hostile Jewish religious leaders, Jesus made this claim about Himself: "You study the Scriptures diligently because you think that in them you have eternal life. These are the very Scriptures that testify about me" (John 5:39 NIV).

Jesus was saying that what we call the Old Testament, which Jewish people at the time considered their scriptures, contained prophecies and other teachings that pointed to Him as their long-awaited Messiah. Jesus was the one God had promised to send, the Savior who fulfilled everything the Lord had spoken through the Old Testament prophets.

Though Jesus' Jewish opponents had dedicated their lives to studying the Old Testament, they didn't recognize Him as the fulfillment of all they had read. What Jesus told them shows us today that we should read and study *all* of scripture, not just the New Testament, to truly know Him.

Jesus came from heaven to live as a man on earth, to teach and preach like no one ever had before, to perform amazing miracles that proved who He really was, to die on a cross to pay the price for our sins, and to be raised from the dead to show us that He had power over sin and death.

It was just as the Old Testament prophets had said.

# The Good News

The first four books of the New Testament—Matthew, Mark, Luke, and John—contain the story of Jesus' life. Together, they are called the *Gospels*, a word meaning "good news." But the good news of salvation through Jesus Christ didn't start with His arrival on earth. It began several centuries earlier with the "messianic prophecies" scattered throughout the Old Testament.

For example, the book of Isaiah, written around seven hundred years before Jesus' birth, contains so many prophecies of the coming Messiah that some Christians call it "the fifth Gospel." Almost one-third of Isaiah's sixty-six chapters contain prophecies about the birth, life, and death of Jesus, or about His return to earth in the end times. In fact, Isaiah provides more detail about the second coming than any other Old Testament prophet.

Isaiah's first messianic prophecy is that Jesus would be born to a virgin and called Immanuel (Isaiah 7:14). Matthew 1:23 provides a translation: "God with us." Isaiah's best-known prophecy, perhaps, is that Jesus "was wounded for our transgressions, He was bruised for our iniquities. The chastisement of our peace was on Him, and with His lashes we are healed. We all like sheep have gone astray. We have turned, each one, to his own way, and the LORD has laid on Him the iniquity of us all" (53:5–6).

Isaiah predicted that the Messiah would make the blind see, the deaf hear, the mute speak, and the lame

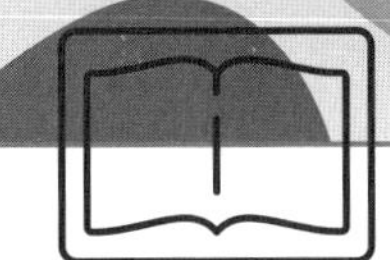

# Approximate Dates in the Life of Jesus

- 4 or 5 BC—His birth
- 4 or 5 BC—Journey to Egypt with His family
- 3 or 4 BC—Return from Egypt
- AD 8—Boyhood visit to the temple
- AD 26—The ministry of John the Baptist
- AD 26—Baptized by John the Baptist
- AD 26—First year of His ministry (year of inauguration)
- AD 27—Second year of His ministry (year of popularity)
- AD 28—Third year of His ministry (year of opposition)
- AD 29 or 30—Year of His death

walk (Isaiah 35:5–6). The Gospels include many accounts of Jesus performing healing miracles, as well as other miracles such as turning water into wine, feeding thousands of hungry people with a small amount of food, walking on water, and calming storms. Each case demonstrated Jesus' powerful, divine nature.

Here is a list of Jesus' miracles in the order they happened and where you can read about them in the Bible:

1. Changing water to wine at the wedding at Cana (John 2:1–11)
2. Curing the nobleman's sick son (John 4:46–54)
3. The great catch of fish (Luke 5:1–11)
4. Casting out an unclean spirit (Mark 1:23–28)
5. Healing Peter's mother-in-law of a fever (Mark 1:30–31)
6. Healing a man of leprosy (Mark 1:40–45)
7. Healing the centurion's servant (Matthew 8:5–13)
8. Raising a widow's son from the dead (Luke 7:11–17)
9. Stilling a violent storm (Matthew 8:23–27)
10. Healing two demon-possessed men (Matthew 8:28–34)
11. Healing a paralyzed man (Matthew 9:1–8)
12. Raising a synagogue leader's daughter from the dead (Matthew 9:18–26)

13. Curing a woman of an issue of blood (Luke 8:43–48)

14. Opening the eyes of two blind men (Matthew 9:27–31)

15. Loosening the tongue of a man who could not speak (Matthew 9:32–33)

16. Healing a severely disabled man at the pool called Bethesda (John 5:1–9)

17. Restoring a man's shriveled hand (Matthew 12:10–13)

18. Healing a demon-possessed man (Matthew 12:22)

19. Feeding five thousand men with a small amount of food (Matthew 14:15–21)

20. Healing a Canaanite woman's daughter (Matthew 15:22–28)

21. Healing a deaf and mute man (Mark 7:31–37)

22. Feeding four thousand men with a small amount of food (Matthew 15:32–39)

23. Giving a blind man sight (Mark 8:22–26)

24. Curing a boy who was plagued by an evil spirit (Matthew 17:14–21)

25. Opening the eyes of a man born blind (John 9:1–38)

26. Curing a woman who had been afflicted for eighteen years (Luke 13:10–17)

27. Curing a man of a condition called dropsy (Luke 14:1–4)

28. Cleansing ten men with leprosy (Luke 17:11–19)

29. Raising Lazarus from the dead (John 11:1–46)

30. Giving two blind men sight (Matthew 20:30–34)

31. Causing a fig tree to wither (Matthew 21:18–22)

32. Healing the ear of the high priest's servant (Luke 22:50–51)

33. Rising from the dead (Luke 24:5–8)

34. A second large catch of fish (John 21:1–14)

# Jesus' Traveling Ministry

During His three-year ministry on earth, Jesus visited many places. It has been estimated that He and His disciples walked a total of more than three thousand miles. The places Jesus visited are important due to the things He did and said in them. Here are fifteen such places and why they matter:

1. **Bethany**: A village about two miles from Jerusalem. This was the home of three siblings, Jesus' close friends Lazarus, Martha, and Mary. Bethany was the site of one of Jesus' most famous miracles, raising Lazarus from the dead (John 11). Six days before the Last Supper, Jesus went to Bethany and had dinner at the home of Simon the Leper. There Mary anointed Jesus with oil (John 12:1–8). After His triumphal entry into Jerusalem, Jesus stayed at Bethany.

2. **Bethsaida**: A town on the northeast edge of the Sea of Galilee where Jesus healed a blind man. In a desert place near the city, Jesus preached to a crowd, then fed them—five thousand men, not counting women and children—with the loaves and fish of a boy's lunch (Matthew 14:15–21). After this, Jesus sent the disciples on to Bethsaida by boat, then walked to them on the water.

3. **Cana**: A Galilean village where Jesus and His disciples attended a wedding and the Lord performed His first miracle by turning water into wine. The family hosting the wedding had run out of wine, so Mary, Jesus' mother, informed her son of the need. Jesus told servants to fill six large stone jars with water. When the water was drawn out again, it was a fine wine (John 2:6–10).

4. **Capernaum**: A village on the Sea of Galilee's northern shore, chosen by Jesus as His ministry headquarters. He left Nazareth for Capernaum when Herod imprisoned John the Baptist (Matthew 4:12–17). Here Jesus taught in the synagogue, and He called several disciples—fishermen Peter, Andrew, James, and John, and the tax collector Matthew. He also performed many miracles.

5. **Decapolis**: A territory defined by a confederation of ten cities settled by the Greeks, Decapolis was largely southeast of the Sea of Galilee. People from this area were among the crowd that followed Jesus early in His ministry. Jesus healed a deaf and mute man here (Mark 7:32) and also miraculously fed four thousand men (Mark 8:1–9).

6. **Egypt**: An often-powerful nation southwest of Israel, in the northeastern corner of Africa. Following Jesus' birth, God commanded Joseph to take Mary and the Baby into Egypt to escape the jealous rage of King Herod. After Herod's death, God recalled the family to Israel (Matthew 2:13–21).

7. **The region of the Gaderenes**: The name Gadara doesn't appear in scripture, only the name of its people. Here Jesus healed a man with a legion of unclean spirits who lived among the tombs. Having seen this miracle, the Gadarenes requested that Jesus and His disciples leave their land (Luke 8:26–39).

8. **Gethsemane**: A garden across the Kidron Valley from Jerusalem, on the Mount of Olives. Jesus brought His disciples to Gethsemane where He prayed, asking the Father to take the cup of crucifixion from Him. Despite His deep sorrow, Jesus accepted His Father's will, while His nearby disciples, Peter, James, and John, fell asleep. An armed crowd arrived to arrest Jesus, following Judas' betrayal by a kiss. The disciples fled as their Master was led away to face the Jewish ruling council, the Sanhedrin (Matthew 26:36–57).

9. **Jerusalem**: Jesus first visited this important city as an infant, when He was dedicated at the temple. The Bible also describes another visit, for Passover, when Jesus was twelve years old. Here Satan tempted Jesus as a young man to throw Himself down from the temple. Early in His ministry, Jesus visited Jerusalem and taught at the temple. But because the religious and civil leaders rejected His message and even sought to kill Him, He did not spend large amounts of time in the city. As Jesus headed toward Jerusalem in His final days, He recognized that His death had to take place in the city. Jesus was arrested outside Jerusalem, tried within it, and crucified, and buried just outside the city, at Golgotha.

10. **Mount Hermon or Mount Tabor**: Scholars believe one of these two mountains is where Jesus took His disciples Peter, James, and

John to witness the transfiguration. When Jesus and the three men descended the mountain, He performed another miracle: healing the demon-possessed son of a man who pleaded for help after the other nine disciples failed to heal the boy. Jesus used this event to teach His followers the importance of prayer and fasting (Mark 9:1–29).

11. **Nain**: A Galilean village. As Jesus and a crowd of followers came to the city gate, a funeral procession for a young man was coming out. Jesus had compassion on the man's mother, a widow, and brought her son back to life (Luke 7:11–15).

12. **Nazareth**: In this village of Galilee, the virgin Mary heard the news that she would bear the Messiah. Here Jesus announced the beginning of His ministry and the fulfillment of the promise of good news and liberty for God's people. The faithless people of His hometown were angry at this, and tried to kill Jesus (Luke 4:28–29). Matthew reports that their unbelief caused Jesus not to do many miracles there (Matthew 13:58).

13. **Samaria**: In New Testament times, Samaria was a Roman province between Galilee and Judea. On the border between Samaria and Galilee, Jesus healed the ten leprous men, only one of whom gave thanks. At Sychar, a place where Jacob had dug a well centuries

earlier, Jesus discussed spiritual matters with a Samaritan woman. He told her that He was the Messiah she'd been awaiting (John 4:4–26).

14. **The Temple**: Shortly after His birth, Jesus was brought to the temple in Jerusalem so His parents could offer a sacrifice. Here Simeon and the prophetess Anna recognized God's salvation in Jesus. After their return to Nazareth, Joseph and Mary went to Jerusalem each year for Passover. When Jesus was twelve, He was found in the temple, talking with the teachers of the law. At one point in His ministry, Jesus cleared the temple of the cattle, sheep, and doves that were sold for sacrifice, declaring, "Do not make my Father's house a house of business" (John 2:16).

15. **Tyre and Sidon**: People from this area followed Jesus when they heard of the remarkable things He was doing. When He received little response from the people of Israel where He had done many of His miracles, He cried out that Tyre and Sidon would have humbly repented. In this area, a Syrophoenician woman called on Jesus to cast an evil spirit from her daughter. Because of the mother's persistence, Jesus obliged (Matthew 15:21–28).

# World-Changing Teaching

As Jesus traveled around Israel, He not only performed miracles but spoke life-changing truths. Jesus communicated by way of important sayings, powerful sermons, and memorable stories called parables.

Here are twenty-five of the most important things Jesus said:

1. "I say to you, ask, and what you ask for will be given to you. Look, and what you are looking for you will find. Knock, and the door you are knocking on will be opened to you. For everyone who asks, will receive what he asks for. Everyone who looks, will find what he is looking for. Everyone who knocks, will have the door opened to him" (Luke 11:9–10 NLV).

2. "See! I stand at the door and knock. If anyone hears My voice and opens the door, I will come in to him and we will eat together" (Revelation 3:20 NLV).

3. "If anyone wants to be first, he must be last of all. He will be the one to care for all" (Mark 9:35 NLV).

4. "For sure, I tell you, whoever does not receive the holy nation of God as a little child does not go into it" (Mark 10:15 NLV).

5. "Do not say what is wrong in other people's

lives. Then other people will not say what is wrong in your life. You will be guilty of the same things you find in others. When you say what is wrong in others, your words will be used to say what is wrong in you" (Matthew 7:1–2 NLV).

6. "I am the Bread of Life. He who comes to Me will never be hungry. He who puts his trust in Me will never be thirsty" (John 6:35 NLV).

7. "Whoever drinks the water that I will give him will never be thirsty. The water that I will give him will become in him a well of life that lasts forever" (John 4:14 NLV).

8. "For sure, I tell you, unless a man is born again, he cannot see the holy nation of God" (John 3:3 NLV).

9. "For God so loved the world that He gave His only Son. Whoever puts his trust in God's Son will not be lost but will have life that lasts forever" (John 3:16 NLV).

10. "This, then, is how you should pray: 'Our Father in heaven, hallowed be your name, your kingdom come, your will be done, on earth as it is in heaven. Give us today our daily bread. And forgive us our debts, as we also have forgiven our debtors. And lead us not into temptation, but deliver us from the evil one'" (Matthew 6:9–13 NIV).

11. "All power has been given to Me in heaven and on earth. Go and make followers of all the nations. Baptize them in the name of the Father and of the Son and of the Holy Spirit. Teach them to do all the things I have told you. And I am with you always, even to the end of the world" (Matthew 28:18–20 NLV).

12. "Do not gather together for yourself riches of this earth. They will be eaten by bugs and become rusted. Men can break in and steal them. Gather together riches in heaven where they will not be eaten by bugs or become rusted. Men cannot break in and steal them. For wherever your riches are, your heart will be there also" (Matthew 6:19–21 NLV).

13. "Do for other people whatever you would like to have them do for you. This is what the Jewish Law and the early preachers said" (Matthew 7:12 NLV).

14. "No one can serve two masters. Either you will hate the one and love the other, or you will be devoted to the one and despise the other. You cannot serve both God and money" (Matthew 6:24 NIV).

15. "Watch out! Be on your guard against all kinds of greed; life does not consist in an abundance of possessions" (Luke 12:15 NIV).

16. "I tell you, there will be more joy in heaven because of one sinner who is sorry for his sins and turns from them, than for ninety-nine

people right with God who do
not have sins to be sorry for"
(Luke 15:7 NLV).

17. "Come to me, all you who are weary and burdened, and I will give you rest. Take my yoke upon you and learn from me, for I am gentle and humble in heart, and you will find rest for your souls. For my yoke is easy and my burden is light" (Matthew 11:28–30 NIV).

18. "If anyone wants to be My follower, he must give up himself and his own desires. He must take up his cross and follow Me. If anyone wants to keep his own life safe, he will lose it. If anyone gives up his life because of Me and because of the Good News, he will save it" (Mark 8:34–35 NLV).

19. "You have heard that it has been said, 'You must love your neighbor and hate those who hate you.' But I tell you, love those who hate you. (Respect and give thanks for those who say bad things to you. Do good to those who hate you.) Pray for those who do bad things to you and who make it hard for you" (Matthew 5:43–44 NLV).

20. "I give you a new Law. You are to love each other. You must love each other as I have loved you. If you love each other, all men will know you are My followers" (John 13:34–35 NLV).

21. "The most important one," answered Jesus, "is

this: 'Hear, O Israel: The Lord our God, the Lord is one. Love the Lord your God with all your heart and with all your soul and with all your mind and with all your strength.' The second is this: 'Love your neighbor as yourself.' There is no commandment greater than these" (Mark 12:29–31 NIV).

22. "For sure, I tell you, if you have faith as a mustard seed, you will say to this mountain, 'Move from here to over there,' and it would move over. You will be able to do anything" (Matthew 17:20 NLV).

23. "If you forgive people their sins, your Father in heaven will forgive your sins also. If you do not forgive people their sins, your Father will not forgive your sins" (Matthew 6:14–15 NLV).

24. "I am the Way and the Truth and the Life. No one can go to the Father except by Me" (John 14:6 NLV).

25. "But seek first his kingdom and his righteousness, and all these things will be given to you as well" (Matthew 6:33 NIV).

## *The Parables*

Both Psalm 78:1–3 and Isaiah 6:9–10 predicted that the Messiah would teach in parables. A parable is a story told to create a picture in people's minds to help them understand some greater spiritual truth. Jesus told many parables to teach people about Himself or the nature of His kingdom.

Here is a list of Jesus' parables, complete with scripture references:

1. The Parables of New Cloth and New Wineskins (Matthew 9:16–17; Mark 2:21–22; Luke 5:36–38)
2. The Parable of the Lampstand (Matthew 5:14–16; Mark 4:21–22; Luke 8:16)
3. The Parable of the Wise and Foolish Builders (Matthew 7:24–27; Luke 6:47–49)
4. The Parable of the Sower (Matthew 13:3–23; Mark 4:3–20; Luke 8:5–15)
5. The Parable of the Weeds (Matthew 13:24–30, 36–43)
6. The Parable of the Mustard Seed (Matthew 13:31–32; Mark 4:30–32; Luke 13:18–19)
7. The Parable of the Leaven (Matthew 13:33; Luke 13:20–21)
8. The Parables of the Hidden Treasure and the Pearl (Matthew 13:44–46)
9. The Parable of the Net (Matthew 13:47–50)
10. The Parable of the Homeowner (Matthew 13:52)
11. The Parable of the Wandering Sheep (Matthew 18:12–14)

12. The Parable of the Unmerciful Servant (Matthew 18:23–31)

13. The Parable of the Workers in the Vineyard (Matthew 20:1–16)

14. The Parable of the Two Sons (Matthew 21:28–32)

15. The Parable of the Tenants (Matthew 21:33–44; Mark 12:1–11; Luke 20:9–18)

16. The Parable of the Wedding Banquet (Matthew 22:1–14)

17. The Parable of the Fig Tree (Matthew 24:32–35; Mark 13:28–29; Luke 21:29–31)

18. The Parable of the Ten Virgins (Matthew 25:1–13)

19. The Parable of the Talents (Matthew 25:14–30; Luke 19:12–27)

20. The Parable of the Sheep and the Goats (Matthew 25:31–46)

21. The Parable of the Growing Seed (Mark 4:26–29)

22. The Parable of the Returning Owner (Mark 13:34–37)

23. The Parable of the Moneylender (Luke 7:41–43)

24. The Parable of the Rich Fool (Luke 12:16–21)

25. The Parable of the Watchful Servants (Luke 12:35–40)

26. The Parable of the Wise and Foolish Servants (Luke 12:42–48)

27. The Parable of the Unfruitful Fig Tree (Luke 13:6–9)

28. The Parable of the Master and the Servant (Luke 17:7–10)

29. The Parable of the Good Samaritan (Luke 10:30–37)

30. The Parable of the Friend Seeking Bread (Luke 11:5–8)

31. The Parable of the Place of Honor (Luke 14:7–11)

32. The Parable of the Great Banquet (Luke 14:16–24)

33. Parables About Counting the Cost (Luke 14:28–33)

34. The Parable of the Lost Sheep (Luke 15:3–7)

35. The Parable of the Lost Coin (Luke 15:8–10)

36. The Parable of the Prodigal Son (Luke 15:11–32)

37. The Parable of the Shrewd Manager (Luke 16:1–9)

38. The Parable of the Rich Man and Lazarus (Luke 16:19–31)

39. The Parable of the Persistent Widow (Luke 18:2–8)

40. The Parable of the Pharisee and the Tax Collector (Luke 18:10–14)

## Jesus' Ultimate Mission

During His three years of traveling around Israel teaching and performing miracles, Jesus knew that His ultimate purpose on earth was to give Himself up to die, to shed His blood so that people could be forgiven for their sins.

Matthew 21–27, Mark 11–15, Luke 19–23, and John 12–19 record several important events that occurred during the week of Jesus' death. He continued His teaching in Jerusalem that week, including what is called the "Olivet Discourse," describing the end times and the signs of His second coming (Matthew 24–25; Mark 13:1–37; Luke 21:5–36). Jesus met with His disciples for the Passover meal, an event known as the "Last Supper" (Matthew 26:17–30; Mark 14:12–26; Luke 22:7–38). After the meal, Jesus led the disciples to the Garden of Gethsemane to pray as He anticipated what lay ahead (Matthew 26:36–56; Mark 14:32–52; Luke 22:40–53; John 18:1–11). Then Jesus was arrested and taken into custody. He would be interrogated by the chief priests, the Roman governor Pontius

# Jesus' Seven Statements from the Cross

1. Pleading on behalf of His tormenters: "Father, forgive them, for they do not know what they are doing" (Luke 23:34 NIV)
2. Praying to God the Father: "Eli, Eli, lema sabachthani?" (which means "My God, my God, why have you forsaken me?") (Matthew 27:46 NIV)
3. Speaking to the penitent thief on the cross: "Truly I tell you, today you will be with me in paradise" (Luke 23:43 NIV)
4. Speaking to His mother: "Woman, here is your son." Speaking to the disciple He loved: "Here is your mother" (John 19:26–27 NIV)
5. "I am thirsty" (John 19:28 NIV)
6. "Father, into your hands I commit my spirit" (Luke 23:46 NIV)
7. "It is finished" (John 19:30 NIV)

Pilate, and King Herod (Luke 22:54–23:25).

Matthew 27:2–56, Mark 15:33–41, Luke 23:27–56, and John 19:16–36 all describe Jesus' crucifixion and death. Before He was nailed to the cross, Roman soldiers tortured and mocked Jesus. John 19:2–3 says the soldiers "wove a crown of thorns and put it on His head, and they put a purple robe on Him and said, 'Hail, King of the Jews!' And they struck Him with their hands."

Forced to carry His own cross, Jesus was led away to a place called Golgotha (or Calvary), where Roman soldiers fixed Him to the wooden crossbar. Then He was lifted up for all to see. Crucified with a criminal on either side of Him, Jesus' first words from the cross were, "Father, forgive them, for they do not know what they do" (Luke 23:34).

Around noon, a strange darkness covered the land. Later, Jesus cried out to God the Father, "Eli, Eli, lama sabachthani?"—that is to say, "My God, My God, why have You forsaken Me?" (Matthew 27:46). When the time came for Jesus to die, He cried out "It is finished" (John 19:30), and "Father, into Your hands I commend My spirit" (Luke 23:46). Having said that, Jesus released His spirit and died.

Miraculous things happened at the moment. For one thing, "the veil of the temple was torn in two from the top to the bottom" (Matthew 27:51), a visual indication that a new way had been opened into God's presence.

Matthew 28:1–10, Mark 16:1–8, Luke 24:1–12, and John 20:1–10 all describe Jesus' resurrection from the dead. This was the fulfillment of a prophecy Jesus Himself had made to His disciples: "We are going up to Jerusalem, and the Son of Man will be delivered over to the chief priests and the teachers of the law. They will condemn him to death and will hand him over to the Gentiles to be mocked and flogged and crucified. On the third day he will be raised to life!" (Matthew 20:18–19 NIV).

Jesus' words echoed those of Old Testament prophecies stating that the Messiah would die but come back from the dead (Psalm 16:9–11; 118:17–18). His death on the cross was horrible. But His resurrection was a joyful event that truly changed the world.

# Studying and Memorizing the BIBLE

After reading this far, you may be thinking that the Bible is really an amazing book. You might even be thinking, *I want to know more about the Bible and what it should mean to me as a girl who loves Jesus.*

If that sounds like you, great! Christians of all ages should want to know God's written Word better, to apply it to their everyday lives. But you can't expect that to happen by osmosis. You'll have to put in some real effort, making Bible reading, study, and memorization a regular part of your faith life.

Scripture tells us of "Berean Jews" who "were of more noble character than those in Thessalonica, for they received the message with great eagerness and examined the Scriptures every day to see if what Paul said was true" (Acts 17:11 NIV). Commit yourself to being like those Berean Jews, ready to study the Bible every day so you can really take hold of its truths. Along the way, you'll grow in your faith, enough to help your friends and relatives who need some Bible-based wisdom and encouragement.

The best reasons for reading, studying, and memorizing the Bible are found in, well, *the Bible itself.* Here are several:

**To help make you secure in your own salvation**: Many Christians go through times of doubt about their own salvation. Through learning portions of scripture that address our personal salvation, we can find assurance and comfort. That's partly what Paul meant when he wrote to his young friend and coworker Timothy, "You have known the Holy Writings since you were a child. They are able to give you wisdom that leads to being saved from the punishment of sin by putting your trust in Christ Jesus" (2 Timothy 3:15 NLV).

**To help you grow in your faith**: In 1 Corinthians 3:1 (NLV), Paul called new believers "baby Christians." All babies need nourishment to grow and develop. That includes baby Christians, who need spiritual nourishment, which Peter called "the pure milk which is God's Word" (1 Peter 2:2 NLV). The Bible repeatedly refers to itself as food for the soul.

**To receive personal blessing and encouragement**: Many believers go through times of discouragement in their faith lives. When you study the Bible, you'll read many promises God made to give you hope. You'll also read stories of how God worked in the lives of people to rescue them, bless them, and encourage them.

**To receive personal guidance**: You probably aren't faced with the same kinds of life issues as your parents or other adults, but you're sure to face important decisions that lead you to wonder, *What should I do now?* Learning the Bible is helpful in answering this question. "Your Word is a lamp to my feet and a light to my path" (Psalm 119:105 NLV). Many times, the Bible addresses a specific situation, but when it doesn't, there are still many principles you can apply to your life. You can have confidence when you're being led by God's Word.

**To defend ourselves against the devil**: Soon after we become Christians, we learn that the Christian life involves what is called "spiritual warfare." In Ephesians 6, Paul instructs believers with these words: "Put on the full armor of God, so that you can take your stand against the devil's schemes" (verse 11 NIV). Those schemes are the methods Satan uses against people, trying to keep them from doing God's will. One vital part of this armor is "the sword of the Spirit, which is the word of God" (verse 17). Through study and memorization, you'll be able to remember specific verses and, by applying them, to overcome the devil's tricks and schemes.

**To help you overcome sin**: Psalm 119:11 (NLV) says, "Your Word have I hid in my heart, that I may not sin against You." The psalmist understood that the Word of God, the Bible, helps us to overcome temptation. Jesus was the perfect example of someone who'd hidden God's Word in His heart. When the devil tried to tempt Him, Jesus defeated that temptation by responding with God's Word (Matthew 4:1–11).

## Bible Study Tools

Studying the Bible for yourself involves hard work. Fortunately, many resources can help with the process.

**Study Bibles**: Over the years, many knowledgeable men of God have developed study Bibles. They typically include the whole text of the Bible along with study notes and other materials. Barbour Publishing's *KJV Study Bible* and *Light for Life NASB Study Bible* are examples.

**Bible dictionaries and encyclopedias**: These references, which can often be found online, include definitions of words, as well as helpful explanations and scripture references related to a subject. *The New Unger's Bible Dictionary*, *Zondervan's Pictorial Bible Dictionary*, and *The International Standard Bible Encyclopedia* are all excellent resources. Barbour's *Practical Bible Dictionary* includes both concise dictionary entries and concordance entries for the most important words and phrases. (See an explanation of concordances below.)

**Concordances**: These resources list references where important biblical words are found. An exhaustive concordance includes every word in scripture, while other concordances emphasize more important key words. If you remember only a single word or a phrase from a verse, a concordance will help you find its reference. It's important to make sure the concordance you select is keyed to the Bible translation you're using.

**Topical Bibles**: These books list biblical words alphabetically, providing select references to the location of the word you're studying. Use this resource when you're doing word or character studies.

**Expository dictionaries**: These study aids examine the original Hebrew and Greek words used in Bible verses, along with brief definitions and explanations.

**Atlases**: If you want a more detailed description of biblical geography, along with explanatory articles, seek out a book like *The Barbour Bible Atlas*. Atlases contain many more maps than those that typically appear in the backs of Bibles.

**Commentaries**: Using these books is like being taught by great men and women of God. Some commentaries explain individual verses and analyze how they fit together. They also generally include an outline of the Bible book under consideration. Other commentaries are devotional in nature, emphasizing lessons for Christian living. *The Layman's Bible Commentary—Old Testament* and *The Layman's Bible Commentary—New Testament* are examples.

**Online resources**: If you don't have access to printed study tools, a quick online search will lead you to good Bible dictionaries, commentaries, concordances, and anything else a girl needs to study the Bible in-depth for herself. Excellent resources include biblegateway.com, studylight.org, and biblestudytools.com.

## Inductive Bible Study

The tools listed above will help you to engage in what is called "the inductive Bible study method." This method guides you toward discovering facts and details in a Bible text, then drawing conclusions about the meaning of a text from those observations. Inductive study includes three components:

- **Observation** answers the question, *What does it say?* What is the actual content in the text?
- **Interpretation** answers the question, *What does it mean?* Our task is to discover the original intent and meaning of the author.
- **Application** answers the questions, *What does it mean to me?* and *How does it apply to my life?*

When you follow this study method, then you'll be able to interpret the Bible correctly. That means you'll receive from God everything He intended when He gave you His written Word. Here's how inductive Bible study works:

## Observation

Before you can consider what a Bible text *means*, you must ask what it *says*. This means reading and rereading a text until you become acquainted with it, then observing what it really says through a series of questions. Biblical texts will have answers for most of the following questions:

- ***Who?*** Who was writing? To whom was the message originally written? Who are the people involved?
- ***What?*** What's happening? What's said? Is it a command, an exhortation, a rebuke, a question, an answer, a prayer, a quotation of other

scripture, something else? What's the main point? What key words or phrases are used?

- ***When?*** Are there time references? Are there words related to the past, present, or future? Look for words like *after*, *until*, and *then*.
- ***Where?*** Are there locations mentioned—towns, roads, rivers, mountains, regions, or other landmarks?
- ***Why?*** Are there any clues about why things are being said or done?
- ***How?*** Is there an explanation about how things are done?

These six questions help us gain information to see what a text actually says.

## *Interpretation*

The ultimate interpretation question is, *What did God mean by what He said?* Interpretation is determining the meaning of a text once all of the facts are in. Compiling evidence from our observation takes some time, and we must guard against jumping to premature conclusions. New evidence can influence your conclusions, so you must take your time and use the study resources as you move through this part of the inductive process.

## *Application*

The third and final step in the inductive Bible study process is figuring out what the text means to you. Bible study doesn't end with observation and interpretation but continues to the question *So what?* The goal of Bible study isn't only gaining information but experiencing transformation and enjoying God's blessings. We're not just trying to get through the Bible; we're letting the Bible get through us. If there's a good example, follow it. If there's a warning, heed it. If there's a command, obey it. If there's a promise, believe it.

## Reading Through the Bible

One of the best ways to start your Bible study journey is to just read. Start at Genesis 1:1 and go all the way through to the last verse of Revelation. This will take some time, and there will be parts of the Bible that are difficult to plow through. But reading the entire Bible will give you a good foundation for more in-depth studies later on.

If you want to read the Bible from cover to cover, an organized plan will help. You can find several good reading schedules online from websites like bibleplan.org.

## Studying Bible Books and Passages

You can apply the inductive method of Bible study to both whole Bible books and shorter passages. As you study books and sections of books, pay close attention to the characters and what they did and said, how God responded, and the lessons you can learn.

Here are thirty great passages for study:

1. **Genesis 1–3**: Creation and the entrance of sin
2. **Genesis 6:9–8:22**: The flood
3. **Exodus 20:3–17**: The Ten Commandments
4. **Joshua 1**: God's instructions to the new leader of Israel
5. **1 Samuel 17:12–54**: David's battle with Goliath
6. **1 Kings 8:12–54**: Solomon's prayer dedicating the temple
7. **Psalm 1**: The blessed man
8. **Psalm 23**: God as our shepherd
9. **Psalm 91**: God as our source of safety and security
10. **Psalm 139**: God knows you well
11. **Isaiah 6:1–8**: The prophet Isaiah's call
12. **Daniel 3:8–30**: Shadrach, Meshach, Abed-nego, and the fiery furnace
13. **Daniel 6**: Daniel in the lions' den
14. **Luke 2:1–20**: The birth of Jesus
15. **Matthew 3:13–4:11**: Jesus' baptism and temptation

16. **Matthew 5–7**: Jesus' Sermon on the Mount
17. **Matthew 22:34–40**: Jesus' teaching on the greatest commandment
18. **Matthew 27:27–28:10**: Jesus' death and resurrection
19. **Luke 11:2–4**: The Lord's Prayer, a model for us
20. **John 3:1–21**: New birth in Jesus Christ
21. **John 4:1–42**: The Samaritan woman at the well
22. **Acts 2**: Believers receive the Holy Spirit
23. **Romans 8**: Life through the Holy Spirit
24. **Romans 12**: Christians as living sacrifices
25. **1 Corinthians 13**: The Bible's "love chapter"
26. **Ephesians 4**: Unity and maturity in the body of Christ
27. **Philippians 2:1–18**: Imitating Jesus' humility
28. **Hebrews 11**: The "Faith Hall of Fame"
29. **James 1**: Overcoming temptation and hardship
30. **1 Peter 1**: Hope and holiness

# Word Studies

It's no exaggeration to say the Bible is filled with important, life-changing words. These words can help you grow in your life of faith as you increase in understanding of God. Want some examples? How about *grace*, *faith*, *forgiveness*, *salvation*, *love*, *mercy*, *sin*, *repentance*, and *holiness*, just to name a few?

Studying individual words in scripture can give you a deeper knowledge and better understanding of your Christian faith. The Bible is a treasure chest filled with beautiful truths and promises awaiting your discovery.

## *Seven Steps to Doing a Bible Word Study*

1. Choose a word for study.
2. Using a regular dictionary, find words that mean the same thing (synonyms) and words that mean the opposite (antonyms).
3. Look up the word in a Bible dictionary and jot down references.
4. Look up the scriptures in your Bible and compare the verses to one another.
5. Compile notes, writing out the biblical definition of the word based on your study.

6. Pray and ask God to reveal His truth and meaning of the word
7. Ask yourself, "What does this word mean to me, and how can I apply it to my faith life?"

## Character Studies

The Bible includes the accounts of literally hundreds of men and women—some who served God faithfully, some who struggled in their life of faith, and some who didn't follow the Lord at all.

Whether they were good people or bad, God has given us the opportunity to learn from them. We can find inspiration and encouragement, as well as warnings about what *not* to do, in the lives of Bible characters.

When you begin a study of a Bible character, use a Bible dictionary or an online Bible search (Biblegateway.com is an excellent resource) to find every passage where that person's name is mentioned. That makes it easier to take notes on what is said about the person.

Earlier in this book, in chapter 2, you saw a list of fifty important people in the Bible. Let's take a closer look at just one of those people: Peter, a key character in the New Testament. The following is information you can extract from the Bible about the leader of Jesus' twelve disciples:

- Name: Peter (also known as Simon Peter, Simon, and Cephas)
- Meaning of name: Rock

- Family life: Nothing is known for sure about Peter's birth. He had a brother named Andrew, who was also a disciple and introduced him to Jesus.
- Occupation: Peter was a fisherman without much education or biblical training (Acts 4:13). Jesus called him and others to be "fishers of men" (Matthew 4:19).
- Strengths: Peter was a passionate follower of Jesus. After receiving the Holy Spirit, he preached the sermon at Pentecost, and three thousand believed (Acts 2).
- Weaknesses: Peter was headstrong and sometimes spoke before he thought (Mark 8:32–33; 9:5). He sometimes tried to tell Jesus what to do! Peter even scolded Jesus for suggesting that He was going to die in Jerusalem (Matthew 16:21–23).

## *Important acts and events in Peter's life:*

- Calling of Peter (Matthew 4:18–22)
- Walking on water (Matthew 14:28–33)
- Affirms Jesus as Messiah (Mark 8:29; Matthew 16:16)
- Scolds Jesus, who strongly rebukes Peter (Matthew 16:21–23)
- Witnesses the Transfiguration (Matthew 17:1–13)
- Denies Jesus three times (Matthew 26:69–75)

- Reinstated by Jesus (John 21:15–19)
- Preaches at Pentecost (Acts 2)
- Heals a lame man (Acts 3)
- Stands up to the authorities (Acts 4–5)
- Realizes the gospel is also for Gentiles (Acts 10–11)
- Raises Dorcas from the dead (Acts 9:40)
- Writes 1 and 2 Peter

## *Lessons from Peter's story:*

As you read Peter's story, ask yourself these questions and any others that come to mind:

- What did Peter do well?
- What did Peter not do well?
- What does Peter's story teach about saying what we think?
- What does Peter's story teach about dealing with failure?
- How did the Holy Spirit change and empower Peter?
- What does Peter show us about relying on the Holy Spirit?
- In what ways should I be like Peter?

## Topical Bible Studies

Topical Bible study is the study of—you guessed it—various topics covered in the Bible. This type of study involves looking up Bible passages that address the topic at hand and finding out everything the Bible has to say about it. For example, if you wanted to study the topic of *love*, you'd go to John 3:16, John 15, Romans 5:5–11, Romans 8:35–39, 1 Corinthians 13, Galatians 5:22–25, Ephesians 2:1–10, Ephesians 3:14–21, 1 John 4:7–21, and other related passages. Read, meditate, and write down everything the Bible says about what love is, how God loves you, and how you can love others.

## Bible Memorization

Whether you know a lot about the Bible or you're new to scripture, memorizing verses can help you tremendously in your faith life. For example, if you're trying to share your faith with another person, verses like John 3:16, Acts 4:12, Romans 10:9–10, and Ephesians 2:8–9 would be great to be able to quote. Or if you're having a tough day—or you know someone else who needs encouragement—it's good to have ready verses such as

Psalm 42:11, Isaiah 40:31, 2 Corinthians 4:16–18, and 1 Peter 1:3–4.

You might want to pick out a verse to memorize and read it over and over until you can quote the text, chapter, and verse without needing to look at your Bible. Or you could write a verse on paper over and over until you have it fixed in your memory. You might write verses on note cards to review as you have a free moment, or put that information on your phone.

Bible memorization is great on your own, but even better with a partner—a friend, a sibling, or a parent. You can quiz each other and hold each other accountable.

Find the method that works best for you. . .then memorize!

## *66 Great Verses to Memorize—One from Each Bible Book*

1. Genesis 15:6
2. Exodus 20:3
3. Leviticus 11:44
4. Numbers 14:18
5. Deuteronomy 6:5
6. Joshua 24:15
7. Judges 7:2
8. Ruth 1:16
9. 1 Samuel 15:22
10. 2 Samuel 7:18
11. 1 Kings 18:37
12. 2 Kings 2:9
13. 1 Chronicles 17:14
14. 2 Chronicles 6:14
15. Ezra 7:10
16. Nehemiah 5:19
17. Esther 2:15
18. Job 1:21
19. Psalm 121:1–2
20. Proverbs 3:5
21. Ecclesiastes 12:1
22. Song of Songs 2:4

23. Isaiah 53:6
24. Jeremiah 18:6
25. Lamentations 3:22
26. Ezekiel 18:32
27. Daniel 9:18
28. Hosea 11:4
29. Joel 2:32
30. Amos 4:12
31. Obadiah 17
32. Jonah 2:9
33. Micah 6:8
34. Nahum 1:7
35. Habakkuk 2:4
36. Zephaniah 3:17
37. Haggai 2:4
38. Zechariah 1:3
39. Malachi 3:7
40. Matthew 7:7
41. Mark 1:17
42. Luke 12:34
43. John 3:16
44. Acts 4:12
45. Romans 8:28
46. 1 Corinthians 13:1
47. 2 Corinthians 5:21
48. Galatians 5:22–23
49. Ephesians 2:8–9
50. Philippians 4:6
51. Colossians 3:2
52. 1 Thessalonians 4:16
53. 2 Thessalonians 3:13
54. 1 Timothy 1:15
55. 2 Timothy 2:3
56. Titus 3:5
57. Philemon 4–5
58. Hebrews 12:1–2
59. James 5:16
60. 1 Peter 5:8
61. 2 Peter 3:9
62. 1 John 4:7–8
63. 2 John 6
64. 3 John 4
65. Jude 3
66. Revelation 5:12

## ***Fifty Great Scriptures to Memorize***

All verses from the New International Version.

1. **2 Timothy 3:16–17**: All Scripture is God–breathed and is useful for teaching, rebuking, correcting and training in righteousness, so that the servant of God may be thoroughly equipped for every good work.

2. **John 3:16–17**: "For God so loved the world that he gave his one and only Son, that whoever believes in him shall not perish but have eternal life. For God did not send his Son into the world to condemn the world, but to save the world through him."

3. **Proverbs 3:5–6**: Trust in the LORD with all your heart and lean not on your own understanding; in all your ways submit to him, and he will make your paths straight.

4. **Galatians 2:20**: I have been crucified with Christ and I no longer live, but Christ lives in me. The life I now live in the body, I live by faith in the Son of God, who loved me and gave himself for me.

5. **John 14:6**: Jesus answered, "I am the way and the truth and the life. No one comes to the Father except through me."

6. **Romans 3:23**: For all have sinned and fall short of the glory of God.

7. **Romans 6:23**: For the wages of sin is death,

but the gift of God is eternal life in Christ Jesus our Lord.

8. **Isaiah 53:5**: But he was pierced for our transgressions, he was crushed for our iniquities; the punishment that brought us peace was on him, and by his wounds we are healed.

9. **Romans 5:8**: But God demonstrates his own love for us in this: While we were still sinners, Christ died for us.

10. **Colossians 2:13–14**: When you were dead in your sins and in the uncircumcision of your flesh, God made you alive with Christ. He forgave us all our sins, having canceled the charge of our legal indebtedness, which stood against us and condemned us; he has taken it away, nailing it to the cross.

11. **Romans 10:9–10**: If you declare with your mouth, "Jesus is Lord," and believe in your heart that God raised him from the dead, you will be saved. For it is with your heart that you believe and are justified, and it is with your mouth that you profess your faith and are saved.

12. **1 John 1:9**: If we confess our sins, he is faithful and just and will forgive us our sins and purify us from all unrighteousness.

13. **2 Corinthians 5:17**: Therefore, if anyone is in Christ, the new creation has come: The old has gone, the new is here!

14. **Philippians 1:29**: For it has been granted to you on behalf of Christ not only to believe in him, but also to suffer for him.

15. **Proverbs 18:10**: The name of the LORD is a fortified tower; the righteous run to it and are safe.

16. **1 Peter 1:6–7**: In all this you greatly rejoice, though now for a little while you may have had to suffer grief in all kinds of trials. These have come so that the proven genuineness of your faith—of greater worth than gold, which perishes even though refined by fire—may result in praise, glory and honor when Jesus Christ is revealed.

17. **James 1:2–3**: Consider it pure joy, my brothers and sisters, whenever you face trials of many kinds, because you know that the testing of your faith produces perseverance.

18. **Romans 8:31**: What, then, shall we say in response to these things? If God is for us, who can be against us?

19. **Psalm 56:3**: When I am afraid, I put my trust in you.

20. **2 Timothy 1:7**: For the Spirit God gave us does not make us timid, but gives us power, love and self-discipline.

21. **Philippians 4:6–7**: Do not be anxious about anything, but in every situation, by prayer and petition, with thanksgiving, present your requests to God. And the peace of God, which transcends all understanding, will guard your hearts and your minds in Christ Jesus.

22. **Psalm 46:10–11**: He says, "Be still, and know that I am God; I will be exalted among the nations, I will be exalted in the earth." The LORD Almighty is with us; the God of Jacob is our fortress.

23. **Isaiah 55:8–9**: "For my thoughts are not your thoughts, neither are your ways my ways," declares the LORD. "As the heavens are higher than the earth, so are my ways higher than your ways and my thoughts than your thoughts."

24. **Hebrews 4:12**: For the word of God is alive and active. Sharper than any double-edged sword, it penetrates even to dividing soul and spirit, joints and marrow; it judges the thoughts and attitudes of the heart.

25. **Psalm 1:1–3**: Blessed is the one who does not walk in step with the wicked or stand in the way that sinners take or sit in the company of mockers, but whose delight is in the law of the LORD, and who meditates on his law day and night. That person is like a tree planted by streams of water, which yields its fruit

in season and whose leaf does not wither—whatever they do prospers.

26. **John 1:14**: The Word became flesh and made his dwelling among us. We have seen his glory, the glory of the one and only Son, who came from the Father, full of grace and truth.

27. **Hebrews 11:1**: Now faith is confidence in what we hope for and assurance about what we do not see.

28. **Hebrews 11:6**: And without faith it is impossible to please God, because anyone who comes to him must believe that he exists and that he rewards those who earnestly seek him.

29. **Romans 10:17**: Consequently, faith comes from hearing the message, and the message is heard through the word about Christ.

30. **Ephesians 2:8–9**: For it is by grace you have been saved, through faith—and this is not from yourselves, it is the gift of God—not by works, so that no one can boast.

31. **John 20:29**: Then Jesus told him, "Because you have seen me, you have believed; blessed are those who have not seen and yet have believed."

32. **Psalm 139:23–24**: Search me, God, and know my heart; test me and know my anxious thoughts. See if there is any offensive way in me, and lead me in the way everlasting.

33. **Lamentations 3:22–23**: Because of the LORD's great love we are not consumed, for his compassions never fail. They are new every morning; great is your faithfulness.

34. **Psalm 103:8–10**: The LORD is compassionate and gracious, slow to anger, abounding in love. He will not always accuse, nor will he harbor his anger forever; he does not treat us as our sins deserve or repay us according to our iniquities.

35. **Titus 3:5**: He saved us, not because of righteous things we had done, but because of his mercy. He saved us through the washing of rebirth and renewal by the Holy Spirit.

36. **Psalm 103:1–2**: Praise the LORD, my soul; all my inmost being, praise his holy name. Praise the LORD, my soul, and forget not all his benefits.

37. **Psalm 118:24**: The LORD has done it this very day; let us rejoice today and be glad.

38. **1 Thessalonians 5:16–18**: Rejoice always, pray continually, give thanks in all circumstances; for this is God's will for you in Christ Jesus.

39. **Colossians 3:17**: And whatever you do, whether in word or deed, do it all in the name of the Lord Jesus, giving thanks to God the Father through him.

40. **Psalm 63:1**: You, God, are my God, earnestly I seek you; I thirst for you, my whole being longs for you, in a dry and parched land where there is no water.

41. **John 4:24**: "God is spirit, and his worshipers must worship in the Spirit and in truth."

42. **Romans 12:1–2**: Therefore, I urge you, brothers and sisters, in view of God's mercy, to offer your bodies as a living sacrifice, holy and pleasing to God—this is your true and proper worship. Do not conform to the pattern of this world, but be transformed by the renewing of your mind. Then you will be able to test and approve what God's will is—his good, pleasing and perfect will.

43. **Revelation 4:11**: "You are worthy, our Lord and God, to receive glory and honor and power, for you created all things, and by your will they were created and have their being."

44. **Isaiah 40:31**: But those who hope in the LORD will renew their strength. They will soar on wings like eagles; they will run and not grow weary, they will walk and not be faint.

45. **Galatians 5:22–23**: But the fruit of the Spirit is love, joy, peace, forbearance, kindness, goodness, faithfulness, gentleness and self-control. Against such things there is no law.

46. **Joshua 1:8–9**: "Keep this Book of the Law always on your lips; meditate on it day and

night, so that you may be careful to do everything written in it. Then you will be prosperous and successful. Have I not commanded you? Be strong and courageous. Do not be afraid; do not be discouraged, for the LORD your God will be with you wherever you go."

47. **1 Chronicles 16:34**: Give thanks to the LORD, for he is good; his love endures forever.

48. **Isaiah 9:6**: For to us a child is born, to us a son is given, and the government will be on his shoulders. And he will be called Wonderful Counselor, Mighty God, Everlasting Father, Prince of Peace.

49. **Galatians 4:4–5**: But when the set time had fully come, God sent his Son, born of a woman, born under the law, to redeem those under the law, that we might receive adoption to sonship.

50. **John 16:33**: "I have told you these things, so that in me you may have peace. In this world you will have trouble. But take heart! I have overcome the world."

So there it is! With a bit of planning and consistent effort, you can make scripture a bigger and better part of your life. As you read, study, and memorize the Bible, you'll find that it really is a life-changing book. You'll grow ever closer to God as you go ever deeper into His written Word.

# Also for Teen Girls

The 180 Bible verses in this book will help you identify and attack the enemy called anxiety. Each verse is paired with a devotional thought that is both practical and encouraging. Here you'll find the strength and help you need as your heart is anchored to a solid foundation of faith.

Paperback / ISBN 979-8-89151-256-6